Your Horoscope 2020

· · · · · · · · · · · · · · ·

Gemini

Your Horoscope 2020

·················

Gemini

22nd May - 21st June

igloobooks

igloobooks

Published in 2019
by Igloo Books Ltd
Cottage Farm
Sywell
NN6 0BJ
www.igloobooks.com

0819 001.01
2 4 6 8 10 9 7 5 3 1
ISBN 978-1-78905-713-3

Written by Belinda Campbell and Jennifer Zelinger

Cover design by Dave Chapman
Edited by Bobby Newlyn-Jones

Printed and manufactured in China

CONTENTS

INTRODUCTION
....

This horoscope has been specifically created to allow
you to get the most from astrological patterns and
the way they have a bearing on not only your zodiac
sign, but nuances within it. Using the diary section
of the book you can read about the influences and
possibilities of each and every day of the year. It will
be possible for you to see when you are likely to be
cheerful and happy or those times when your nature
is in retreat and you will be more circumspect. The
diary will help to give you a feel for the specific
'cycles' of astrology and the way they can subtly
change your day-to-day life.

INTRODUCTION

THE CHARACTER OF THE TWINS
··················

Expect a triple dose of conversation, charisma and intellect from Geminians. Not usually satisfied with focusing on one thing at a time, these artful communicators will likely be Tweeting celebrities, texting colleagues and Snapchatting friends simultaneously without even breaking a sweat. Fortunately, they often have twice as much energy as everyone else so won't usually have an issue keeping up with their active social lives. Lively and affable, Geminians are friends, or at least acquainted, with everyone around them. Frequently found fluttering from friend to friend, these social butterflies touch the lives of many.

Geminians crave constant mental stimulation, which is perhaps why they are well known for being intelligent. They are expert conversationalists, and are formidable opponents in a debate. Yet, as much as Geminians are happy to lead or even dominate a conversation, they are also just as eager to listen. To satisfy their eternal curiosity, they can be keen on learning all the facts about a story that has captured their interest, be it serious news or the latest celebrity break-up. This love for knowledge can lead to Geminians learning many secrets, but their athletic approach to conversing could result in them running around and sharing what they've learnt with everyone else. They would be wise to keep any gossiping to a minimum and perhaps apply their knack

for narrative to writing, like fellow Geminians George
Orwell and Salman Rushdie.

THE TWINS

Double the trouble or twice the fun? The Twins that
represent Gemini can be an indication of many, and
sometimes opposing, traits. Castor and Pollux were
half-twin brothers from Greek mythology that have
commonly been portrayed as the Gemini symbol. In
some stories, Castor is thought to be mortal, while
Pollux is immortal. When Castor dies, he is sent to the
Underworld ruled by Hades, leaving Pollux in Olympus
with the Gods. The light and dark of this tale is a
perfect example of the two sides that many Geminians
are commonly thought to display. Their moods are
changeable, which can make them seem duplicitous
or two-faced, while their Mutable quality makes them
advocates of change. Whether it's changing their hair
colour or even their postcode, these fluid beings are
often unrecognisable from one day to the next.
However, Geminians are fascinating characters
to try and get to know.

MERCURY

Orbiting the Sun faster than any other planet in the
Solar System, travel and speed are two associations that
Geminians surely inherit from their ruling planet of
Mercury. Named after the Roman god of communication,
trickery and travel, winged Mercury is a perfect
embodiment of Air sign Gemini. The speed in which we

travel and communicate is ever increasing, much to the joy of quick-thinking Geminians. Feeling the influence of Mercury, they favour instantly gratifying forms of interaction. However, texting, Tweeting and talking rapidly can mean that Geminians may not always think before they speak or press send. 'Mercury in retrograde' is a phrase that is often met with fearful faces, but what does it mean? Three times a year, Mercury seemingly begins to move backwards and is blamed for many communication, media, technology and travel failures. Remember when Geminian Kanye West interrupted Taylor Swift's 2009 MTV Video Music Award speech? That was during a Mercury retrograde!

ELEMENTS, MODES AND POLARITIES

Each sign is made up of a unique combination of three defining groups: elements, modes and polarities. Each of these defining parts can manifest in good and bad ways, and none should be seen to be a positive or a negative – including the polarities! Just like a jigsaw puzzle, piecing these groups together can help illuminate why each sign has certain characteristics and help us find a balance.

ELEMENTS

Fire: Dynamic and adventurous, signs with Fire in them can be extroverted. Others are naturally drawn to them because of the positive light they give off, as well as their high levels of energy and confidence.

Earth: Signs with the Earth element are steady and driven with their ambitions. They make for a solid friend, parent or partner due to their grounded influence and nurturing nature.

Air: The invisible element that influences each of the other elements significantly, Air signs will provide much-needed perspective to others with their fair thinking, verbal skills and key ideas.

Water: Warm in the shallows and freezing as ice. This mysterious element is essential to the growth of everything around it, through its emotional depth and empathy.

MODES

Cardinal: Pioneers of the calendar, cardinal signs jump-start each season and are the energetic go-getters.

Fixed: Marking the middle of the calendar, fixed signs firmly denote and value steadiness and reliability.

Mutable: As the seasons end, the mutable signs adapt and give themselves over gladly to the promise of change.

POLARITIES

Positive: Typically extroverted, positive signs take physical action and embrace outside stimulus in their life.

Negative: Usually introverted, negative signs value emotional development and experiencing life from the inside out.

GEMINI IN BRIEF

The table below shows the key attributes of Geminians. Use it for quick reference and to understand more about this fascinating sign.

SYMBOL	RULING PLANET	MODE	ELEMENT	HOUSE
Ⅱ	☿	⟨•⟩	△	Ⅲ
The Twins	Mercury	Mutable	Air	Third

COLOUR	BODY PART	POLARITY	GENDER	POLAR SIGN
				♐
Yellow, Blue	Shoulders, Arms, Hands, Nervous System	Positive	Masculine	Sagittarius

LOVE
· · · · · · · · · · · · · · · · ·

Like their element Air, Geminians have a lightness to
them that lifts others up. However, anyone who falls for
these flyaway characters will need to work hard to keep
their interests piqued. Geminians can reach dizzying
heights of ecstasy in love but soon lose their curiosity,
leaving partners plummeting back to Earth painfully.
They are likely to have several possible love interests
simultaneously, on multiple different dating apps, but
may be quick to swipe left or abandon conversations if
they get bored. Speed dating could be an interesting
night out for this fast-paced chatterbox!

With a love of change and speed, Geminians may walk
away from relationships too quickly. To hold onto a
relationship, they will need to slow down and take a
moment to honestly discuss whatever issues need to be
mended. Nothing is perfect, and the most worthwhile
endeavours are usually those that take time and effort –
something that Geminians would do well to consider in
their love lives. Whilst they are expert communicators,
taking the time to pause and reflect on problems in a
relationship will probably not come easily, and will be
something they need to work hard at.

Not ones to take themselves too seriously, Geminians
will appreciate energetic lovers that they can have fun
with. Thanks to their Mutable quality, they can be very
easy-going in relationships and are unlikely to fight
for the reigns of control. They usually value partners
who are similarly relaxed, but also could be attracted to

more-forthright types who take the lead and encourage
them to explore new heights. Keep curious Geminians
intrigued and their love will be invigorating.

ARIES: COMPATIBILITY 4/5

Though very different in their approaches to
relationships, these two Positive signs can bring out
the very best in one another. Communication is key for
any relationship, and the Geminian's talkative nature
can help the Arian to vocalise dreams and ideas. These
two can form an intellectual bond that lays a strong
foundation for love. The Twins and Ram are both guilty
of starting projects and not finishing them, which can
extend to their relationship with each other. However,
their similarities and positive natures are likely to still
see them part as friends if the romance extinguishes.

TAURUS: COMPATIBILITY 2/5

Three may prove to be a crowd. The duality of a
Geminian, characterised in the Twin symbol, can
make a Taurean feel uneasy about starting a romantic
relationship. The Earth sign of Taurus mixed with airy
Gemini may not be an easy joining, but if the Taurean
can budge on set ideas then love could grow happily
here. The Geminian's good communication skills help
when understanding the Taurean's needs, providing the
love and security that is craved. Communication, trust
and flexibility should be this couple's mantra if they are
to go the distance.

GEMINI: COMPATIBILITY 4/5

A Geminian couple is likely to be a roaring hit at social gatherings. This pair can share late-night stimulating conversations until the early hours of the morning, and probably still be energised enough to make that brunch date. Life might feel like a constant party when two Geminians unite, but they may struggle to connect deeply on an emotional level. These smart thinkers match each other in many compatible ways, so this relationship will surely be full of shared thoughts and exciting adventures.

CANCER: COMPATIBILITY 2/5

This Air and Water pairing can feel too far apart personality-wise to make a good match, but the differences could actually prove to be strengthening. The Geminian is led by the mind and the Cancerian by emotion. These contrasting perspectives can lead to misunderstandings and arguments if the line of communication isn't clear. The Geminian can help the Cancerian communicate thoughts and feelings aloud rather than keeping them bottled up, while the Cancerian can provide lessons on the value of sensitivity. With so much to learn from one another, understanding and acceptance is vital to their success.

LEO: COMPATIBILITY 4/5

The inner Leonian child can be just what the youthful sign of Gemini asked for. This love can be like a children's story full of love and adventure, think Peter

Pan and Wendy. The high-energy Leonian was born
to lead, whilst the Mutable Geminian is happy to take
this Lion's hand and fly speedily off to Neverland! The
Leonian will encourage the Geminian to take an active
part in the important choices in their lives. Both Positive
signs, their extrovert energies and curious natures will see
this Air and Fire match embarking on endless adventures.

VIRGO: COMPATIBILITY 1/5

A Virgoan may initially be attracted to a Geminian's
charm and wit, but is likely to soon feel irritated by the
flights of fancy. The steady Virgoan can feel too reserved
for the Geminian, and the fast-paced Geminian can
be too unpredictable for the Virgoan. Both ruled by
Mercury and strong believers in communication, these
otherwise contrasting characters may end up feeling as
if they are speaking two completely different languages.
However, their mutual love of change and talent for
adaptability may well be what makes this relationship
last longer than predicted.

LIBRA: COMPATIBILITY 3/5

With Libra ruled by the planet of love, Venus, and Gemini
by the planet of communication, Mercury, this partnership
should be founded on affection and understanding. The
debate-loving Geminian and peace-seeking Libran will likely
have their conflicts. If love troubles do arise, these two will
have a good chance of having the verbal skills and creative
thinking to work out their issues. Both can have trouble
making up their minds, however. The Libran's Cardinal

instinct usually sets in to help make the course of action clear, much to the delight of the Mutable Geminian.

SCORPIO: COMPATIBILITY 3/5

Passionate debates are definitely on the menu for a Scorpian and Geminian in love. The Scorpian's Water element will bring emotional depth to the relationship, whilst the Geminian's Air influence will help breathe a fresh perspective on things. The Scorpian risks suffocating the Geminian with intense emotions if turned toxic. The Geminian can be flirtatious, which can trigger the Scorpian's jealousy, but the Geminian isn't scared of arguing, and actually quite likes the stimulation. Being Fixed, the Scorpian values steadiness so may find the flighty Geminian too unreliable. However, this relationship has the potential to be full of spice and interest.

SAGITTARIUS: COMPATIBILITY 5/5

'I love you just the way you are' could be the vows of a strongly independent Sagittarian and Geminian. Despite both being Mutable and willing to adapt, there is unlikely to be anything about this match that either partner will want to change about the other. Being opposite on the zodiac calendar, the love between the Sagittarian and Geminian is usually always going to be unique. For the easily bored Geminian, the adventurous Sagittarian is a perfect fit, ensuring that this couple has endless days of love and fun ahead.

CAPRICORN: COMPATIBILITY 1/5

This Earth and Air coupling may be an unlikely match, but an awareness of the differences could help create a stronger bond. The Capricornian appreciates the tangible, a good career and beautiful home, whilst the Geminian loves exciting ideas and the invisible workings of the mind. Whilst the Geminian's Mutable element fits well with the Capricornian's Cardinal aspect, what drives the Capricornian may be at odds with the Geminian. This polar-opposite couple – the Capricornian Negative and the Geminian Positive – may struggle to find common ground, but could stand to learn the most.

AQUARIUS: COMPATIBILITY 4/5

An individualist Aquarian and dual-personality Geminian can make for a compatible trio. Born in the eleventh house that signifies community and friendship, the Aquarian thrives in groups and will be a fantastic partner to the social butterfly Geminian. Mutable in nature, the Geminian is happy to follow the Aquarian's Fixed lead, which will likely bring a steadiness to the relationship. Both share the element of Air and are Positive, so are likely to have lots in common. With the Geminian's love of change and the Aquarian's need for progress, these two could create a bright and revolutionary future together.

PISCES: COMPATIBILITY 3/5

As fluid as water and as free flowing as air, a Piscean
and Geminian can experience an extremely flexible and
forgiving relationship if they fall for one another. Both
Mutable, this couple is highly compatible and will not
fight for leadership, but rather rule side by side. Whilst
these two may not always perfectly understand each
other, their open-minded attitudes will help resolve
any disagreements. Whilst the Geminian is led by the
mind-influence of Mercury, contrastingly, the Piscean's
influence of Water means that they can both be ruled by
their emotions. A meeting of the head and heart will
be key.

FAMILY AND FRIENDS

. . . .

'You think you know someone, and then you find out they're a Geminian'. That's the sentiment friends and family of Geminians may express. To truly know Geminians is to be able to identify their light and dark sides, their love of gossip and their passion for politics. Geminians should try to get to know both sides of themselves, just as much as their friends and family should. Their duality means they can be extremely good at acting as go-betweens to friends and families. Able to see two sides to every story, Geminians can act a bridge of communication between two contrasting sides, making them potential peacemakers. Although they may instigate debates that turn into arguments, their knack for seeing multiple perspectives makes them a voice of reason that shouldn't be ignored.

Whether it's about global warming, last night's game or the glass of wine in their hand, Geminians will have an opinion and debate it to the death. Not in it just to win to it, they have endless curiosity, and enjoy being tested as it satisfies their love of learning. Rather than shy away from friends or family who challenge their intellect, stimulating relationships are ones that Geminians will usually try harder to hold on to. Be sure to bring the sparkliest conversation to one of their infamous dinner parties. However, if they fail to be entertained then they will move swiftly on, abandoning a dull conversation and searching quickly for something of more interest elsewhere. Geminians do not attempt to conceal their dwindling interest, so anyone wishing to hold their attention should watch closely – and be ready to change the subject!

Being related to Geminians, who carry the element of Air, can sometimes feel like being caught up in a gale-force wind. Those closest will see them at their stormiest and strongest. Perhaps Geminian Marilyn Monroe best summed it up: "If you can't handle me at my worst, then you sure as hell don't deserve me at my best". Geminians talk non-stop and with endless energy, but if friends and family aren't left exhausted they will no doubt feel enlivened. Their need for constant change, even in relationships, may mean that the dynamics between family and friends constantly evolves and changes too. Having the energy to keep up with Geminians mentally will be a task and a half, but can have exciting rewards. The young energy of Leonians makes them perfect playmates, whilst fellow Geminians are sure to make for more fun.

MONEY AND CAREERS

. . . .

Being a particular star sign will not dictate certain types of career, but it can help identify potential areas for thriving in. Conversely, to succeed in the workplace, it is just as important to understand strengths and weaknesses to achieve career and financial goals.

The planet Mercury is thought to be able to change the way that people think, just like the influential Geminians who are ruled by it. These charismatic characters have a silver tongue, and are more than capable of imprinting their intellect and ideas on those they encounter. They will likely have an aptitude for sales, but sometimes what they sell best is themselves. Kings, queens, prime ministers and presidents, Geminians have been ruling the world for decades. U.S President Donald Trump is just one of the latest in a long line of influential Geminians to make a mark in politics. Strategy, intellect, communication and creating change are all defining features of Geminians and successful leaders. They have a great ability to multitask, so are usually best suited to a career that challenges them intellectually. Therefore, a career in politics is a strong potential avenue.

The youth associated with Mercury gives Geminians an eternal vitality, but could also mean that they are prone to making blunders. Fortunately, they love learning so will usually grow from their mistakes. A teaching environment could be well suited to Geminians. Their ability to communicate and their influential way of thinking could make them favoured teachers amongst pupils. The annual changeover of students would also be a bonus for Mutable Geminians, so long as the lessons themselves aren't too repetitive. They can become bored easily, so will not happily remain in a job that stays the same or prevents them from evolving in some way. Their love of words and narrative could mean that writing is where their talents best bloom, as with Geminian Salman Rushdie.

As with family, colleagues cannot be chosen. Therefore, it can be advantageous to use star signs to learn about their key characteristics and discover the best ways of working together. With the same element of Air, Librans and Aquarians will connect with Geminians on a thoughtful level, and can make inspiring and influential colleagues. Geminian Paul McCartney and Libran John Lennon are a great example of the dizzying heights of success that these two deep-thinkers can help each other reach. Steady Taureans are likely to lock horns with flighty Geminians over their advocacy for change in a work environment. An extra dollop of patience and understanding should be served up if they find themselves on the same team.

HEALTH AND WELLBEING

....

Moved by their element Air, Geminians are full of ideas and insights that will usually be heard loud and clear thanks to their influence of Mercury, the planet signifying communication. Conversely, if they feel like their voices are not being listened to, or are actively being silenced, their health and wellbeing will soon deteriorate. Whilst Mutable Geminians are usually happy to go along with the plans of others, it's integral that they make their imprint in some way if they are to be true to themselves and feel content.

As much as Geminians advocate diversity in their lives, they should similarly celebrate the complicated diversity within themselves. They can be accused of being duplicitous, but their duality is an important part of their uniqueness that they should learn to embrace. Capable of being the life and soul of a party, Geminians can also be prone to feeling overwhelmed, and may experience bouts of depression. Their social sides should be exercised as much as their quieter, thoughtful selves to help maintain emotional balance. Geminians should try to surround themselves with friends and family that allow them to show off their charming face, and challenge their intellect. Ultimately, they should strive to find a balance and avoid feelings of depression by enjoying all sides of their changeable personalities.

Geminians can be eager to move on quickly from things, including their feelings. They like to remain light-hearted, and can be guilty of skimming the surface only. Delving deeply into their emotions might initially feel suffocating to Geminians, however the practice of looking at their deepest emotions and desires can lead them away from living a purely shallow existence. By pausing and focusing more time and energy into themselves and their relationships, Geminians can often twice reap the rewards that they are used to receiving from their more impatient behaviour.

The part of the human body associated with Gemini is the nervous system. It ensures the body acts in the way that the brain tells it to, which is perhaps why communication is so closely connected to this sign. Geminians can push themselves mentally and physically to the point of exhaustion if they choose to ignore signals from their bodies telling them to slow down. However, they will usually only listen to pain before any lasting damage is done. Whilst it is not in their nature to slow down, even energetic Geminians will tire eventually. They may be able to pre-empt a burnout by taking the time to switch off from the constant chatter of their outside life and focus on their internal health. Regular screen breaks and going offline from technology could give their overactive minds a much-needed rest. A peaceful retreat somewhere with terrible phone reception and no internet signal may be just what the doctor ordered.

Gemini

....

2020
DIARY PAGES

JANUARY

Wednesday 1st

Happy New Year! Are you ready for an intense and exciting year ahead? 2020 is one you will certainly remember. This Wednesday gets things started easily enough, allowing you to go slowly should you need to. Make time before bed to enjoy a daydream or two about the future.

Thursday 2nd

Another day is here and Mercury, your planetary guide, is meeting the bigger, better, more-buoyant Jupiter. They meet in your eighth house, magnifying deep emotions and the connections closest to you. Are you ready for a huge revelation? Stay in observation-mode today.

Friday 3rd

This year is not wasting any time, and today brings big stuff to the table. Mars is on the edge of your sixth house asking you to finally act upon bringing your health to the next level. Meanwhile, Mercury wants you to let go of bad habits.

Saturday 4th

Happy Saturday! Mars has entered Sagittarius, and with this your seventh house of relationships. This includes all kinds of relationships including those with friends, your partner or even your colleagues. You should feel excited about what might happen here in the next six weeks.

Sunday 5th

This is an easy and possibly even lazy day, yet you may find yourself feeling somewhat introverted and wanting to retreat. It's perfectly normal as Taurus is in your twelfth house, which tends to make you more reflective and less curious about those around you.

Monday 6th

It is promising to be a more serious day. The Moon activates Saturn and Pluto, the two planets that are highlighted during the next week. It all takes place in your area of intimacy, inheritance, shared resources and power, so it is going to be deep and may go right to your core.

Tuesday 7th

During the next week, Pluto, the agent of transformation, and Saturn, the teacher, will join forces. They are testing you, to help you achieve the greatest transformation you have ever made. Go easy on yourself this Tuesday, and try to take some time off if you can.

Wednesday 8th

Venus, the planet of love, beauty and harmony, is currently in your ninth house of adventure, knowledge and faith. Make this a day to explore your ideas, and that means all of them. Share the results with people you can connect to the most, and from the heart.

Thursday 9th

The Moon is in Gemini, and is also making a harmonious connection to Venus. It is a fabulous Thursday full of love and connection, and you are absolutely in your element and can just enjoy life to the fullest. Focus on the joy. The energy is really high and will peak tomorrow.

Friday 10th

Along with the Full Moon lunar eclipse, the universe brings in massive energy today. Mercury is meeting the Sun, so it is highly likely you will receive new orders right from the king or queen. Something that happens today is important for your transformation, so observe as best as possible.

Saturday 11th

Today still highlights your possessions and values, and this is important for your development. The big news is that with Uranus, the agent of change, moving direct, the planets will move forwards, shifting all areas of your life into uncharted territory. Isn't that exciting?

Sunday 12th

This day has an amazing vibe for you emotionally.
The Moon has entered Leo, and you are keen to
connect with those nearest and dearest to you. There
is also a big meeting taking place between Mercury,
Saturn and Pluto. Today may reveal where your life
is headed.

Monday 13th

The possibilities of life remain exciting. Now the Sun
meets with Saturn and Pluto, while Venus is on her
last day in Aquarius. Whatever you do today, make sure
you meet and connect as much as you possibly can,
and share some love with everyone dear to you.

Tuesday 14th

There is a big shift and a very different energy today.
Venus is now in Pisces, highlighting your career and
legacy sector. She wants you to consider the most
universal, unconditional impact that you can have.
Your emotions turn serious, and you become more
focused on your personal safety and wellbeing.

Wednesday 15th

You realise that you need to check in with yourself first, and make sure you have the perfect grounding before you can start giving to everyone else. What can you do to make your home environment more nurturing and beautiful for you? What do you have around you to make you feel good? Self care is key for replenishing your personal reserves, so take the time for yourself.

Thursday 16th

It is another busy day because Mercury has its final day in Capricorn. You will probably be trying to work out if there is something else needed to make a change happen. The Moon comes into Libra, giving you some fresh air to breathe and the opportunity for a creative day. Make the most of it if you can.

Friday 17th

This is a happy day for you. Mercury is now entering Aquarius, which means your mental activity will peak. With so much excitement, genius ideas and different areas to explore, you will love this energy. Are you ready for a big vision and a stunning adventure ahead?

Saturday 18th

It is a great day to take care of everything you didn't have time for during the week, and the Moon is helping you to focus your energy to get on top of things again. Mercury is locked in a debate with Uranus about your vision and, in particular, how you want to anchor it in the best way possible.

Sunday 19th

This Sunday might not feel as easy as you would like it to, but the energy will ease tomorrow, so you will soon pass through it. You will find a good solution to a health issue, as the Moon has a pleasant conversation with Saturn and Pluto. The solution to your problem might come from someone also, so listen closely.

Monday 20th

Today has such a good vibe! The Moon enters your area of relationships where it meets Mars, helping you to become ready to take action with a friend or a partner. You learn the most from your relationships, so don't spend this day on your own. Make a point of meeting and being with others, enjoy their company and they will enjoy yours.

Tuesday 21st

The Sun joins Mercury in the ninth house, creating excitement, adventure and exploration. The next thirty days are promising to be just the way you like life to be. You may develop an important vision or direction. Just stay curious.

Wednesday 22nd

This Wednesday brings deeper explorations about shared resources, power and transformation. You are once again more seriously involved than you wished to be, but these deeper explorations are of great value. The shift you are making here is tremendous, so dare to dig deep.

Thursday 23rd

Your emotions may become magnified, and you can expect some surprises to pop up. They could be sudden ideas or insights, which may come into your mind during a quiet moment. There are not normally many quiet moments in your life, but if you create space for them you may be surprised what you will find.

Friday 24th

Today's New Moon in Aquarius is a powerful one for you. New Moons are good for making resolutions or for focusing on a theme for the lunar month ahead. One theme highlighted for you is your vision, long-term goals, journeys and adventures.

FEBRUARY

········

Saturday 1st

Today's energy may be lazy to start with, but the arrival of Uranus will soon bring more excitement. If there is any kind of dramatic incident as a result, be sure that it will pass by quickly. Your focus will then turn inwards, giving you a rare opportunity to reflect.

Sunday 2nd

Venus, the goddess of beauty, talks to Uranus, the agent of change, and they agree that your transformation should be beautiful and emphasise your legacy. The reflections in you magnify that too, so there is a real chance you will end the day feeling satisfied.

Monday 3rd

Here comes an energy boost. The Moon enters your sign, so you will be here, there and everywhere, whilst Mercury, your planetary guide, is on his final day in the genius adventure vision mode. The energy will change tomorrow, but for today you can enjoy recharging your batteries.

Tuesday 4th

Today is the start of a two-month period in which Mercury will highlight your career and legacy sector. Use this time wisely to think through how you can make an impact in the world. Elsewhere, Venus and Saturn are meeting for a talk, and it is a good one. You are making steady progress with your transformation.

Wednesday 5th

Mercury is talking to Uranus. Their conversation could be about sudden insights or surprising ideas, but it definitely won't be boring! You are also trying to find a balance between the way you feel and the way you act. Wait before deciding on how best to proceed.

Thursday 6th

It is all about your possessions and belongings today. First, take a look at what you already own. Do you feel grateful for all of it? Next, think about your future. How do you want to handle your money? Is there something you would really like to own?

Friday 7th

The working week ends with some tricky energy. Venus is on her final day in your career and legacy sector, and the Moon is trying to find a balance between your possessions and other people's property. What is fair and what is not?

Saturday 8th

The weekend offers a lot of revitalising energy for you.
The Moon in Leo sparks your communicative expression,
while Venus in Aries enters your sector of friends and
groups. You are likely to have engaging conversations,
meet interesting people and have a good time exchanging
thoughts and hearing all the latest news.

Sunday 9th

This Sunday morning starts with a powerful Full Moon.
It carries a lot of fiery energy because Mars is also
joining the party, and you need to be careful not to run
out of breath. It is good if you interact with others, but
make sure you step back before you feel exhausted. You
may just need a short break before Monday arrives.

Monday 10th

You bring lots of focus to your emotional needs. Tune
into yourself, and try hard to understand what it is that
you really do want and need. Look out for a moment
that will make it easy to let go of something that is no
longer of use.

Tuesday 11th

Tuesday brings an optimistic vibe. You feel good and
may even figure out the right way to make any necessary
improvements. You might have too many ideas at once or
be able to shift perspective very quickly. Everything you
discover today is of equal importance.

Wednesday 12th

There is more Air for you on this Wednesday. The Moon is in Libra, but it is debating with the nodes of the Moon. This means you will want to find creative expression and some fun, but the upcoming changes make it seem impossible. Take a closer look. What are you missing?

Thursday 13th

You will get a better idea about what caused the tension you have been feeling recently. This topic of change and transformation, of becoming more abundant while simultaneously staying grounded, is not simple to achieve, and there are further adjustments to be made. Try to go easy on yourself.

Friday 14th

What you are doing this Friday, is taking care of your day-to-day tasks. That might sound boring, but it will set you up pretty effectively for the next few weeks. Is there something you can change in your daily routine that will help you to generate more power and energy?

Saturday 15th

Mercury, your planetary guide, is slowing down. He is usually full of life, heading from one idea to the next, and this change of pace is affecting you too. You might feel the urge to look more deeply at a particular issue. Just be fine with this, and try not to worry about feeling out of sorts.

Sunday 16th

Mars is now in your area of relationships, and wants to go deeper into the ones that are especially close and intimate. This means the relationships where you share your truth and feel free to be your authentic self. Don't be afraid to go all in.

Monday 17th

Mercury starts his retrograde motion. He has stumbled upon something in your area of career, vocation and legacy, and is ready to think it through in an unusual way. You will find yourself gaining new perspectives, as your overall thought processes will be wired differently during the next three weeks. Just allow that to happen.

Tuesday 18th

Jupiter and Neptune connect with a great energy today, giving you the impulse to dive into the dream realm. You may just have been about to think differently, but you should dream differently instead. With Jupiter and Neptune involved, there are no boundaries to your dreams at all.

Wednesday 19th

The Sun joins Mercury in your career, vocation and legacy sector, and your focus on this area intensifies. Everything that you had thought about will become more tangible during the next thirty days. Combined with the Mercury retrograde, you are onto something big.

Thursday 20th

Today is more serious than you would like it to be.
Some interesting things might happen between you
and a person very close to you. It is also possible that
subconscious thoughts or memories will come to the
surface. Just stay open.

Friday 21st

Friday is even more focused inwards than recent days,
so you should consider starting the weekend early. Take
some time to just be, to listen inside and to let all that
happens in your very close relationships sink into your
mind. Whatever you do, create some space to meditate
and be with yourself.

Saturday 22nd

Finally, the energy feels much lighter to you. The Moon
has just entered your area of travelling, learning and
exploring, so you can use this to maybe search for your
next holiday location. There is still something going on
behind the scenes that could surprise you. It is probably
a good surprise, so are you excited?

Sunday 23rd

The New Moon in Pisces is here. In this lunar cycle, you will have the ability to plant a seed regarding your career, legacy or vocation. With so much energy currently in this area, you will be able to make big changes. Don't forget that you are still looking at things differently, so be prepared to make plans that you may adjust in the near future.

Monday 24th

Venus and Jupiter are having a debate today. Once again, it is about how you handle your friends and social groups, and any changes that are still necessary. How close are you and your friends? Where do you need to draw a line? How much fun is allowed?

Tuesday 25th

Today is pretty intense. Mars is asking for some action to be taken regarding business or your reputation. He is also asking you to let go of something that may have served you well, but that is now no longer in alignment with what you are seeking in your closest relationships.

Wednesday 26th

Massive insights are waiting, or are at least possible. The Aries Moon is able to spark your mind, whilst your planetary guide Mercury holds a meeting with the Sun. What you will probably take away from all of this is the way you wish to approach business, career and legacy in the future.

Thursday 27th

Don't let your emotions spoil the fun. Over the course of the past year, many things have changed, so it is easier to take notice of your feelings. Don't judge how you feel, simply observe your emotions and what they trigger within you.

Friday 28th

Today might feel a bit boring. You may be surprised that you are not up to going out, and will probably even want to spend some time on your own. If you do, it is a good time to relax, enjoy some wellbeing and treat yourself with delicious food.

Saturday 29th

Your focus is still more inwards, but this Saturday is surely not dull. There is a chance your mind is pondering an idea, and you will find an exciting and surprising way to make it happen. However, there is also some tension going on behind the scenes. Perhaps wait until you spread any good news.

MARCH
....

Sunday 1st
It is a Sunday with a good flow, but also one that might
be a little quieter than usual. Overall, you feel quite
happy to just collect your thoughts and get them out
before Monday. If you need to recharge, you will be able
to do so easily.

Monday 2nd
The week starts with a little boost for you. Monday is
the Moon's day, and it is back in Gemini. You can finally
let everything out and connect with people on various
levels. It is a perfect day for any kind of meeting, so
make plans and touch base.

Tuesday 3rd
Today brings tension regarding your big career plans and
changes. What is the necessary action to take now? You
will no doubt have lots of ideas, but which one is perfect?
Wait until the Full Moon arrives, then you will know.

Wednesday 4th

It's another active day, especially for your planetary guide,
Mercury. He arrives back into Aquarius, so your thought
processes might feel much more normal again. There
is still a different angle to how you see certain matters,
however, which may be useful. Mercury also connects to
Venus, bringing in some powerful social connections.

Thursday 5th

Once again the balance between what is yours and what
is others' is highlighted. You feel like you may need to
take some action, but how exactly? Luckily, Venus can
help with an answer. She is entering Taurus, so will
make sure you consider your own value and the value of
possessions effectively.

Friday 6th

Try not to react impulsively this Friday. Just remain
relaxed, take a breath and don't feel intimidated if life
feels a little too much. You can step back if you wish and
just let this day pass by. The weekend is near and it is
much more promising.

Saturday 7th

This is the start of a wonderful weekend. The Moon is in
Leo, which for you means connecting, fun and learning.
You will probably be seen at the hippest party, and will
enjoy the chance to entertain yourself and others. Just
make sure you are not the only one talking.

Sunday 8th

Today could definitely feel cosmic. Expect the unexpected in a very beautiful way. With the Sun hugging Neptune it is a day to dream away. Walk through the world with your eyes wide open, and enjoy all the colours you see and the feelings you experience. Have a blessed Sunday.

Monday 9th

There is another Full Moon, and this time it is the Virgo Full Moon. You will be looking at ways to make changes that align your private life and how the world sees you. This is an important time for you. Be sure to listen to your intuition, as well as to words.

Tuesday 10th

It is a day for celebration, and that is because Mercury, your planetary guide, is moving direct again. You have seen things from a different perspective for long enough, and now life is back to normal. In the next few weeks, you will be able to integrate all that you observed during the retrograde.

Wednesday 11th

The Moon is in your fifth house, making this just the sort of day you like best. It is one that asks for lots of fun and creativity. The Sun is in a happy conversation with Jupiter, so you'll also have lots of good energy. The only thing that could spoil your mind is a lesson about trust, intimacy and sharing.

Thursday 12th

Did you make some changes to your daily routines last month? They would no doubt have benefited you and made life easier if you did. If you didn't, you might want to investigate them again. It is never too late to make changes, so why not do so this Thursday?

Friday 13th

Today is perfect for putting new healthy habits into action. Don't hesitate, just start right away. Whether this is about getting more sleep, watching less television or going for a walk every day, anything that supports your body will ultimately support you.

Saturday 14th

The weekend is here and it is a nice one too. You will find a way to show the world a different side of yourself, which no doubt feels liberating. You are taking action now, at last. Rest assured that it is the right thing to do.

Sunday 15th

Today is great for enjoying time with your significant other or a dear friend. Together you will have lots of fun and laughter, and may even make the most amazing plans. Mercury is about to finish in Aquarius again, so maybe take another look at your travel plans.

Monday 16th

Monday sees Mercury back in Pisces, so you will continue to ponder questions surrounding your career, legacy or vocation. You will likely gather fresh facts and other perspectives in order to piece the puzzle together. Are you curious about what the big picture will look like?

Tuesday 17th

Today is not your average Tuesday. Uranus, the agent of surprises, is in good aspect to the nodal axis, which means you should expect sudden changes to your plans and things just coming to you out of nowhere. It is all likely to be good, so are you ready for the surprises to roll in?

Wednesday 18th

Which side of yourself do you want to show? Will you allow others to get close, or will you draw a line and remove yourself from the situation? There is some intensity available, if you let it happen. Intensity does not always have to be bad, and in this case it is actually very good.

Thursday 19th

The Moon is in Aquarius, so meet with a friend, arrange a family get-together or find other ways to express your vision today. The ideas you offer, be those about yourself or someone else, will be original and unexpected. You will see the surprise on other people's faces when you verbalise your thoughts.

Friday 20th

Happy spring equinox! From here on, the days will be longer than the nights, and nature will sprout and blossom. It is an exciting time, which creates a joy in you to go out and connect. There is also another vibe here, and that is connecting to your inner shadow and bringing some light to it.

Saturday 21st

It is a day to trust your gut and intuition more than your logical mind. Put differently, your logical mind can tune into your intuition today. Isn't that a gift? Trust all your senses, and see what treasure you can bring to the surface that has been hidden from you all this time.

Sunday 22nd

A big shift occurs as Saturn, the teacher, comes into Aquarius for the first time in thirty years. This means his focus is now for you to build a solid vision, and to take all of your ideas and learnings seriously and do something with them. What are your goals? How can you achieve them? Make the most of the opportunity to develop your aims into a tangible plan.

Monday 23rd

The energy around you continues to be potent, but on different levels. While you are still very intuitive, you are also willing to act on your own transformation and change. This is an intense day, so go easy on yourself and just observe whatever comes up.

Tuesday 24th

Here comes another New Moon, this time in Aries. If you can invite your friends to come round and maybe even try and plan some more regular dates in the diary that would be a good thing to do today. Just consider which groups you want to interact with more, and initiate it right away.

Wednesday 25th

You may still be brimming with energy from all your recent conversations with friends. How did they react to your ideas? What could future get-togethers hold? How do you want to interact, and with whom? What can you give to your tribe?

Thursday 26th

Today could be a little tense. You may feel like not talking too much, as unexpected emotions rise up inside of you. You feel uncomfortable with almost everything you encounter, so go home early if possible. Cook some comforting food and step back a little. This will soon pass and you will feel balanced again.

Friday 27th

You may still be feeling friction in the air, so much so that you rename today Friction Friday. Why not change the narrative and make this Fiction Friday, instead? Watch a good movie or box set, maybe a heist or spy caper, and indulge in lots of popcorn and movie snacks. There is no need to take sides in any arguments today.

Saturday 28th

The planets are talking nicely today. In particular, Venus and Jupiter are deep in discussions about ways to expand your most intimate and authentic relationships. Venus wants you to step forwards with all your beauty and love. Will you accept her invitation? It seems like you can only win here.

Sunday 29th

Relief is here, with the Moon entering Gemini. Life will now feel lighter and more exciting, and your mind and emotions will be better aligned. With the Sun already in Aries, you will no doubt be out having a good time from sunrise until sunset.

Monday 30th

Good news! Your planetary guide Mercury is now out of shadow, and that means he is finished with everything that you pondered during the retrograde. It's time for a new venture. Mars is also ready for something new, as he leaves Capricorn behind. You may well like what he is up to next.

Tuesday 31st

Mars moves into your ninth house of travel, foreign cultures, languages and journeys today. On the way in, he meets Saturn to receive instructions. Make sure the actions you take in the next six weeks focus on building a foundation. If you promise to, Saturn will let you pass.

APRIL

Wednesday 1st

Today is certainly a tricky one. No one is a better prankster than you, and you will be able to use all your imagination and wit to create a hilarious April Fool's Day joke. Just be aware that some people may not see the funny side if you go too wild and wacky.

Thursday 2nd

A Leo Moon creates more Fire energy for you, and you will be able to spark and fuel many ideas in yourself and others. Just make it clear to everyone that you will decide in time which fire is the most interesting to you. They are all intriguing, so don't make any promises for now.

Friday 3rd

Friday is Venus day and this one is very special. You should unroll the red carpet for the queen of heavens, love and beauty to enter into Gemini. She will stay for a long time, as she is about to perform a very special transformation. For now, her mission is to beautify you.

Saturday 4th

Saturday is Saturn's day, and today he is talking with Venus to make sure that she receives her mission in full. Meanwhile, Mercury, your planetary guide, embraces Neptune in order to receive the essence of a dream. It is as poetic as it sounds. Indulge in a dream today.

Sunday 5th

Sunday is another special day this week because Jupiter, the planet of expansion, meets with Pluto, the planet of transformation. For you, this means making big progress in your personal development. How you experience intimacy will change during the next six months, as these two will meet again.

Monday 6th

Today solidifies the changes you are going through, and you will start to create some space in your home and family surroundings to allow them to happen. This is a year of major developments for you, and you will feel curious about what may shift. Paint the details in as many colours as you wish.

Tuesday 7th

You will start to get a good insight into what is really happening today. With the Moon in Libra, you can find balance through expressing yourself in creative and fun ways. You might be surprised by the results you see. This is a day to give it a try.

Wednesday 8th

The recent energy peaks with a Full Moon in Libra, as well as a great conversation between Mercury and Jupiter. Fun, joy and your skills are all up for discussion, allowing you to have an amazing day. Just go easy on those who cannot make the most of this energy.

Thursday 9th

Tensions are likely to arise regarding your daily routines. Whilst it may not be the most exciting way to spend time, you should use the next two-and-a-half days to take care of anything you have been putting off. You can get things done here easier than usual.

Friday 10th

Get out your notebook and make an entry for today, April 10th, and everything that is currently happening in your life. Venus, associated with beauty, love and values, is now moving into her shadow phase. She is preparing for a major shift, and will cover the space she is currently walking through again soon.

Saturday 11th

Today brings good news, as the Moon enters your relationships sector while Mercury walks into Aries. This is as an amazing time to connect with friends and partners, or to get involved in all kinds of interaction. Is that music to your ears?

Sunday 12th

Saturn seems to have decided what he wants with this new foundation, because he is giving Mercury some messages to deliver. For you, that means starting to think about the people you want to make this journey with. Nothing is set in stone yet, but you can now start to talk about your plans and see what echoes you receive.

Monday 13th

Monday comes with the third quarter Moon and, once again, you are thinking through your plans. Is there something already there for the taking? There must be something that you are now ready to receive. Look closely and you will surely find it.

Tuesday 14th

Today's energy is just as powerful as yesterday's, however you may be grappling with your emotions. Potential triggers are lurking everywhere. Just make sure to be extra-observant and aware, and do your very best to respond rather than react. It will make all the difference.

Wednesday 15th

Jupiter is making a tense aspect to the Sun. However, something good could still come out of their heated discussion. Jupiter wants to challenge you, and show you that your perception is the key. Try to see a difficult situation from a different point of view. What new insights do you get?

Thursday 16th

It's finally time for a feel-good day! You will feel inspired and free, particularly about your role in your vision, and the travels and journeys you want to take. What foreign things are you curious about, and what would you love to discover?

Friday 17th

You may be preoccupied with thinking about illusions in the outer world. What side are you showing of yourself and who do people expect you to be? Surely the ultimate question is: who do you want to be? There are at least two sides you can show. But which one is most true to you?

Saturday 18th

It is another lovely day to spend time with your friends. Make it one of inspirational talks, storytelling or just plain fun. The most important thing is to connect and communicate. You are surely happy to do that, aren't you?

Sunday 19th

Today asks two different questions. Firstly, are you ready to let your thoughts be followed by actions? Secondly, are you ready to step back a little, and connect to your inside more than to your outside for the next thirty days?

Monday 20th

You may find yourself in a good mood. You are likely to find your own space extremely comforting, and are able to see the value of your own possessions. It is possible you may feel a little out of sorts at times, but those feelings will pass easily as the day continues.

Tuesday 21st

The Sun is debating with Saturn, but this time it is the Sun delivering the message and giving the instructions. Sometimes, actually, frequently, the teacher is also learning. Where in your life are you trying to school somebody? What could you learn from the situation?

Wednesday 22nd

It is a quiet Wednesday, so it is totally understandable if you feel a little flat. Take it easy, and allow yourself the time to rest, meditate and contemplate. You may want to go to a group meditation or a yoga class.

Thursday 23rd

A New Moon in Taurus may not bring the highest energy for you, but it is perfect for grounding. Use this opportunity to start some new habits. With all the recent excitement, you don't want to get lost in a flight of fancy. Try to occupy your body, and not just your mind. It will help you immensely.

Friday 24th

You will find yourself in a great place today, with your values and the way you act upon them becoming perfectly aligned. That is not always the case, so embrace it. Maybe have a little celebration, or connect to a friend or partner. Together, you can just enjoy the harmonious flow of energy.

Saturday 25th

You've missed something. There is something fundamental that you have not yet considered about power, your own power or the power that is needed to transform yourself. Or did you perhaps give your power away? How will you get it back? Today brings you insight.

Sunday 26th

Sunday message: The recent issue about power has to be rethought. That is what Pluto is thinking as he starts his retrograde motion. Power structures, deep connections, trust. All these things are brought to the table and will be reviewed again, over the next five to six months.

Monday 27th

Your focus will become directed more inwardly, as Mercury, your planetary guide, arrives in Taurus and into your twelfth house. Today could actually be a rather exciting start to the working week, and a big surprise could well be waiting for you.

Tuesday 28th

Something is hanging in the air this Tuesday. It is the last time you can make adjustments to your possessions, or at least the focus of them. Is there something you think you need in your life? If you believe in the idea of a perfect moment, this is it.

Wednesday 29th

So what do you think now, about your possessions and shared possessions? What is the thing you maybe never wanted to share, but now do? How is this experience different to the way you imagined it to be? These are just some of today's interesting questions.

Thursday 30th

The month ends on a happy note, well at least the latter part of today does. Before that, Saturn asks you to find a balance through your emotions. You will find that your immediate surroundings play a big part in your mood and approach to the world. How and where can the balance be found?

MAY

. . . .

Friday 1st

The overall energy today is silent, yet powerful. You are
focused on yourself and the journey of your life. You may
suddenly receive a major insight, and your challenge will
be how to act upon it accordingly. It may be wise not to
act, and to tune into your feelings instead.

Saturday 2nd

You will tend to know exactly what to do today, which
will help you to be very productive. Get out a pen and
paper and write a to-do list. Tackle each job one at a
time and cross them off your list as you go. This will give
you a very grounded and safe feeling.

Sunday 3rd

Take a look at your financial situation and the choices
that you have to make. A retreat or holiday that allows
you plenty of time to yourself might be a good idea.
Before you book, be sure to fully consider your budget.

Monday 4th

You want to incorporate more balance and harmony into your life, and today you can consider what parts of yourself have kept you from achieving that, thus far. There is probably some adjustment necessary to make that happen, but it will be much easier than you might currently think.

Tuesday 5th

You will reach a major shifting point as the north node enters Gemini. For the next eighteen months, your focus will be on your self-development, personality, vitality, will and how you are perceived by others. You will be asked to prioritise your own desires and needs before you invest in relationships of any kind. Invest in yourself first and foremost.

Wednesday 6th

The Moon is in your sixth house, and is once again asking you to focus on how you can support your own health, and how you can connect to your body. It would be helpful if you could do something where you feel your body intensively. This could be through dancing, spinning, running or swimming. Push yourself and you will feel the rewards.

Thursday 7th

Yesterday, you looked at ways to become more physically active. It is, however, also important to create space for regeneration. This could be through healthy eating or through practices like meditation, t'ai chi or qigong. You need both activity and regeneration to be in perfect balance.

Friday 8th

This is the first time that the Moon has crossed the new south node in Sagittarius. For you, this may manifest as the first real test of your needs and wants versus someone else's. It could be your mate, a business partner or a friend. Stay true to yourself, and don't feel forced to compromise just to maintain false harmony.

Saturday 9th

You are asked to transform your thoughts about money, and to communicate openly and trustfully with others about it. Make sure you are heard and understood correctly. You are seeking a new kind of stability, while simultaneously raising the bar on what you value the most. This is necessary because your interests have changed.

Sunday 10th

Now that you have identified your new values and needs
and are asking for them to be met, Jupiter wants to
bring you real abundance with it. Consider it possible
to both trust and receive from others, and you will be
surprised by how easily things will manifest in your life.

Monday 11th

Saturn's first exploration in Aquarius is ending and he
turns retrograde. You have already begun to consider
which horizons you want to expand, what you want
to learn, and where you wish to travel. It is time to
reconsider these plans and recreate some structures
before you can move ahead.

Tuesday 12th

Today sees a homecoming for Mercury into Gemini. This
means you will be in your element. You won't be able
to get enough of talking, writing or communicating in
any way, shape or form. However, don't get lost in the
superficial or idle gossip. There should be a moment of
silence and listening in every day.

Wednesday 13th

Venus retrograde takes place in your first house today.
As you might have realised, you are being subjected
to several different energies. You are on the brink of
a complete makeover. During the retrograde, you may
want to consider how you can express yourself in the
most beautiful way.

Thursday 14th

As the Moon reaches its last quarter square to the Sun, you will start to ask yourself how you can move forwards in a more grounded kind of way. How can you be physically present in the world without getting stuck, whilst still remaining flexible in your thoughts and beliefs?

Friday 15th

There's never a dull moment right now. The latest development is Jupiter retrograde. This means your ability to expand will start to recalibrate. Take a closer look at what you already have, and at all the treasures that may still be buried beneath the surface.

Saturday 16th

Your emotions are in conflict with public demand today. You need some boundaries, and it is possible that you need to make those very clear. Otherwise, people might just occupy your space and time more than they usually do. Don't take this lightly. Stand up for yourself and your own needs.

Sunday 17th

A beautiful day, as the Sun is in trine with Jupiter. This is a lucky day and you could consider buying a lottery ticket. Despite being retrograde, Jupiter might want to bless you with money or something else that you find valuable.

Monday 18th

Your mind is ready to communicate with everybody, and your hands are willing to do all the tasks necessary. You are full of energy, and are able to achieve everything on your to-do list as your mind and emotions are aligned. Recognise and honour this wisely.

Tuesday 19th

The way you relate to friends is at the forefront of your mind. Will your current makeover affect your relationships? The answer to that question is, yes. However, be reassured by the fact that all the people who belong in your life will still be there once you are done with your transformative dance.

Wednesday 20th

Another major shift occurs today, as the Sun enters Gemini. It's your birthday time now, so take a look back at the previous year of evolution, before returning your thoughts to what is happening now. How will this help your future to unfold? Write down what you want to have accomplished by next year.

Thursday 21nd

You will most likely feel tired, sluggish or maybe even a bit lazy today. That's fine. The Moon is in its darkest phase, so this is a good time to take a break and recharge your batteries. The New Moon ahead will prove to be important, so rest while you can.

Friday 22nd

Happy New Moon in Gemini! The support you receive from the universe is incredible today. If you want to get your message across fully, plant your seeds wisely this lunar cycle. They will come to fruition and connect to many cycles during the next eighteen months.

Saturday 23rd

You have many thoughts running around in your head, probably too many for now. You don't know which ideas to act upon, and may even be doubting your own abilities to make things happen. Don't lose yourself in doubt. Instead, focus on what you have already been analysing for a while.

Sunday 24th

How do you feel about yourself? Do you feel good? Do you think that people get your point of view? It is important that you think about your emotions, your message and your own perspective. Trust that there are people receiving you with care and love.

Monday 25th

Usually, you think everything through. This is a day that focuses solely on your emotions. Try to recognise your true feelings about yourself and your self-love. Allow yourself time and space to let these feelings rise up, and also allow time to process each one.

Tuesday 26th

It is another day of deep emotions, as you encounter a person close and dear to you. If you dare to show your innermost feelings, you will allow a new emotional depth and trust between the two of you. You don't need to be afraid. Just open your heart to love.

Wednesday 27th

It is a great day to express yourself, and you know you can do this best while talking to your friends. Maybe invite them to the park. If you feel more like being alone, go to the park by yourself and take a pen and paper with you to capture any inspiring ideas.

Thursday 28th

Mercury has rushed through Gemini, and is now entering your area of self-love, talents, capacities and possessions. You will have plenty of time to consider this area of your life in a completely new way. For now, just know that your mind is opening up to your heart and feelings.

Friday 29th

This Friday is about home, family and roots. This could mean visiting family members this weekend, or it could be you getting more structured and sorted at home. With Mercury now in this area, there will at least be talks or calls coming up.

Saturday 30th

Is there something regarding communication with your family members that you want to change? Are you unsure as to the best way to approach it? Just try something and see how the response goes. Maybe this is actually about showing your true self, rather then telling stories all the time.

Sunday 31st

Usually, you love the Moon in Libra. It highlights your sense of creativity and your creative expression, after all. This month, the beauty and benefits of the Moon are even stronger, so just make sure you express yourself fully and without hesitation. Express yourself straight from the heart.

JUNE
. . . .

Monday 1st
The recent creative and expressive vibe continues today.
You can apply it in all areas of your life, even in career
and business. If there are any projects you are involved
in, you will have the ability to raise them to the next
level and push them forwards.

Tuesday 2nd
Your own needs are likely to be in conflict with the
demands of the world today. You may want to step
back and have time by yourself, but you will need to be
visible, and to be seen and heard publicly. There is no
hiding today, so just show up and make the best of it.

Wednesday 3rd
The Moon is opposing Uranus, so this is another day
that will take you out of your comfort zone. You may be
surprised by the feelings and thoughts that suddenly
pop up in your mind. It might be difficult to grasp what
is really happening, but as time passes everything will be
revealed to you.

Thursday 4th

There is some tension today and it might occur in the act of trying to balance your needs with those of your partner. Just try to stay observant and respond instead of reacting. This gives you the best possible chance to act from a loving position, and to resolve every issue easily. There is no need for conflict if you can avoid it, and keep sailing smooth.

Friday 5th

Happy Full Moon in Sagittarius! This Full Moon highlights your relationships and partnerships. You will be asked to find new ways of relating, first to yourself, and then to others. You are working hard on your self-love, and this should be reflected in your relationships with others as well.

Saturday 6th

You will have a strong need to feel as much as you can in your relationships today. Lately, you may have fallen for the illusion of the perfect partnership, and painted a vivid image of it in your mind. However, you must also consider reality and the limitations it brings. Try to find the middle ground. Perfection may be overrated, and reality has its own benefits to bring.

Sunday 7th

You are still pondering your emotions and your urge for more intimacy. You are eager to find grounding and some kind of anchor in this area. To be able to find it, you need to be in alignment with yourself, and not be afraid to expose your desire.

Monday 8th

It is a great start to the week, as the energy shifts from highly transformative to optimistic. You feel that you can take responsibility for your feelings, and are capable of increasing their intensity and depth. The key here is to open up, while still maintaining healthy boundaries.

Tuesday 9th

Today feels much lighter as the Moon shifts into Aquarius. You may have amazing ideas and find a great flow for sharing them with the groups and communities you are involved in. Make sure you are out and active, because this is not a day to stay at home on the sofa. *Carpe Diem* - Seize the day!

Wednesday 10th

Today's energy is interesting, as it once again forces you to confront the disharmony between outer demands and your inner world. What if you can dream the perfect balance into being? What if all you need to do is trust that it is possible? Take some time to engage with your dreams and visions.

Thursday 11th

The universe does not tire of trying to explore the conflict between your innermost self and public life. Today, you will begin to process the topic on a more emotional level. You will benefit from taking notes, as well as making a new entry in your diary.

Friday 12th

Did you write in your diary yesterday? No? Do it now instead. If you have any old journals, this is an amazing day to flip through them. It will allow you to see how much you have changed throughout the years, and you will surely find some reoccurring themes.

Saturday 13th

This is a powerful day. Your feelings become fully aligned with your motives and the actions you take. If you ever wanted to support a charity or accept an honorary appointment, this would be the day to do so. You want to be of service to the world, so how are you going to do it?

Sunday 14th

There is a good amount of positive and progressive energy available to you today, and you can make the best use of it by seeing your friends. This is also a great day to invest time in new projects, and for gathering ideas for future endeavours.

Monday 15th

Your mind and emotions are in conflict today. Emotionally, you just want to push forwards, but your thoughts bring up all kinds of resistance. 'Should I be more careful?' and 'Do I need to protect myself?' are just two of the questions you are pondering. Listen to your heart.

Tuesday 16th

There is a feeling of release with today's energy. You are absolutely allowed to make this a sensual day. If you do, speak to all five senses. You can include aromatherapy, a bath or massage, your favourite food, a walk out in nature or the sound of the music you love.

Wednesday 17th

Make this a day filled with pleasure. Sometimes, you need to go easy on yourself and step back. You can recharge and collect your thoughts in this solitude, so that you can communicate more directly when you return to the outside world.

Thursday 18th

Mercury, your planetary guide, starts its retrograde motion in Cancer. You will reconsider and recalibrate your possessions, money, self-love and talents. You have already begun to open up from your heart, so now it is time to check in with your feelings even more deeply.

Friday 19th

Another powerful day begins, as the Sun crosses the north node. It is likely that you will remember today, and that some of the events that occur will foreshadow your future. You are currently working on the north node, and will continue to do so for around the next five years. You are literally reinventing yourself.

Saturday 20th

Today's energy requires you to act in a much bigger way in your career, or for your legacy, than you would normally considered doing. Now that the time has come, you will see that it is easy to do as long as you remain compassionate. Your actions will most likely be appreciated.

Sunday 21st

The universe has arranged a major reset, starting with the New Moon solar eclipse at the summer solstice. Look around you and see everything that is familiar. Now close your eyes for a moment. When you open them again, look at your surroundings as if through new eyes.

Monday 22nd

How do you feel today? Your emotions are highlighted even more, now that the Sun and Moon are in Cancer. Questions you could ask yourself are: what do I want to invest in? How is my emotional state mirrored in my surroundings? What can I do to support myself?

Tuesday 23rd

Are there children in your home, family or friendship group? You might want to connect with them today, and be inspired by their curiosity and honesty. You might also feel encouraged to share some of your stories, which would be highly appreciated.

Wednesday 24th

Now that Neptune is retrograde, it is a great time to engage more with your dreams by starting a dream journal. This includes your nightly dreams, as well as your daydreams. You have the power to imagine things into being, and this skill may prove very useful in the future.

Thursday 25th

You made it through the Venus retrograde, which was particularly demanding on you. However, just as a caterpillar must go through a transformation to become a butterfly, you too need to work very hard on yourself. All your efforts will pay off, and you will soon be able to spread your wings.

Friday 26th

Today is another reminder for you to take the right actions. Regarding you and your partnerships, there has to be a perpetual balance and stability. The key to achieving this is to focus on yourself first, even if that scares you. If you do, you will be able to give to others more openly and freely.

Saturday 27th

This is the final day of Mars in Pisces and, once again, your emotional responses are highlighted. Which do you consider to be more important: home or family? Are you actually able to realise a dream or are you thinking too big? Your responses could feel uncomfortable, but these questions have to be asked to allow you to move forward with your goals.

Sunday 28th

Lots of active energy will be available for you now, and for a long time to come. 2020 is a year of intensity, but there is magic taking place in all of the shifts, work and growth. In the meantime, you can focus on making the most of this energy by spending time with your favourite friends.

Monday 29th

Your creative expression is highlighted today, and you will try to accommodate a number of things. Structure, expansion and transformation are just some of the keywords. As you create, try to break old structures and think about new ways to express yourself. Maybe you can even transform something old into something new, and surprise yourself in the process.

Tuesday 30th

A major event is taking place in the universe. It is the second meeting of Pluto and Jupiter. You will wonder how you can open up your heart more optimistically, and not fall into trust issues. If you can transform the way you relate, you will be able to bring about something new.

JULY
....

Wednesday 1st
Another important day is dawning as Mercury meets
with the Sun. It is likely you will have new insights
about how to handle your mind regarding your self-
love. Specifically, this could concern the way you speak
to yourself. Have you ever told yourself 'I love you'?
Do it today.

Thursday 2nd
As Saturn moves back into Capricorn, a distinct focus
is put back onto your life. It is for the greater good, as
it will allow you to lay down the structures needed to
achieve a more stable future. You need to find the right
place to anchor before you can explore.

Friday 3rd
The Moon is in Sagittarius, and is highlighting your
one-to-one relationships. It is a great day to spend some
time with your partner or a close friend. You might want
to go to a restaurant or to hear a lecture. Just be sure to
choose a place where you can enjoy lively conversation.

Saturday 4th

The energy is ramping up, and again highlights your commitments. Are you willing to commit to a relationship, a person or even a location? You like to be involved in many things at once, but what if you actually dare to dedicate yourself to just one thing?

Sunday 5th

A Full Moon lunar eclipse in Capricorn normally spells intensity, and your focus will shift strongly to your intimate connections today. You may also take a closer look at matters relating to money, possessions and inheritance. It is likely that the answers will be revealed over time, and not immediately. Be patient, all will become clear eventually.

Monday 6th

After the intensity of the Full Moon, some much-needed Air energy becomes available to boost your mood. There is also a feeling of momentum, as you receive clarity regarding your individuality and self-realisation. There is still work to be done, but you are getting closer every day. You can do this, all progress is good progress.

Tuesday 7th

Your sense and will to communicate is heightened today, helping you to connect with all sorts of different people. You will enjoy different perspectives and viewpoints, and will want to learn more about other cultures and traditions. All this may result in you booking your next holiday.

Wednesday 8th

You will long to be assertive in projects and groups today, but your feelings will keep getting in the way. Try not to judge your emotions, and just allow them to be. Everyone will benefit from you stepping up, so have the confidence to do so.

Thursday 9th

You will need your new sense of self-love and acceptance to make yourself seen and heard. You usually have no hesitation in talking, but this is about something of importance and you may feel uncomfortable in the spotlight. Trust yourself, and love yourself. You can handle it.

Friday 10th

Today you feel great, and in sync with yourself and the world. It would be an ideal day to go swimming or spend time by the sea or a lake. Make it a fun day, with water splashes, your favourite sundae and an ice-cold drink.

Saturday 11th

Hopefully, you will be in good company this weekend, as company is exactly what you are seeking. Your preference is to be with a whole group of friends, rather than just one person. You may even decide to throw a party for everyone you know.

Sunday 12th

Mercury retrograde is over. The first question is: how do you feel? How do you feel about yourself? Have you been able to stop some of the judgemental thoughts you've been having? You now have more time to integrate your new beliefs fully.

Monday 13th

The Moon returns to Taurus, and this should tell you it is time to step back, create space for yourself and do something that honours your senses. You could buy yourself a bouquet of flowers, for example, or one of your favourite scented candles. A nice meal would be another option.

Tuesday 14th

This day is asking you to find balance and healing. The balance concerns what you invest in yourself versus what you invest in others, whilst the healing concerns a wound you have surrounding the role you play in a particular group. Trust yourself to discover a way forwards.

Wednesday 15th

The energy is still high, as today's task is to find a balance between the way you have always acted, and the way you should act going forwards. You want to transform how you manage and handle issues, and have already made some of the changes necessary. You are getting closer to the core of the matter.

Thursday 16th

The recent energy eases as the Moon enters Gemini. The only thing to be aware of is this: you are not your mind. You sometimes become so distracted by your thoughts you forget that fact. You are actually much more, so remember to also consider your heart and emotions.

Friday 17th

It's time to meet with your closest friends and tell them about the changes you have recently made. Ask them to just listen and let you do all the talking, and promise that you will return the favour very soon. It is important to process everything that has happened, and talking is the best way to do so.

Saturday 18th

Throughout a huge part of the day, you will still be in the mood for communicating and sharing. You may go and meet with family or speak on the phone. One of these talks may offer you a surprising insight, and give you another piece of the bigger puzzle.

Sunday 19th

The Moon joins Mercury, and this will bring your thoughts and feelings into alignment. You will feel nurtured and loved, and may want to cook an amazing lunch or dinner. Be sure to invite lots of guests along to the feast, as you will really enjoy playing the host.

Monday 20th

Today's New Moon in Cancer is all about anchoring an emotional stability and structure. Once you have found a solid approach to self-love, you will be able to restructure your intimate connections. You will be working on this topic for a while, and today is a great day to set an intention.

Tuesday 21st

It's time for creativity! What about your writing projects? When did you last pick up a pen? You might want to do this today, or even start a new venture. You should at least collate a few ideas, because you might be ready by tomorrow to shift the story towards a new vibe.

Wednesday 22nd

The Sun enters Leo, and this again boosts your self-expression and storytelling skills. Have you ever considered writing about your life? Maybe this is something that you could do now, as you are shifting and changing. Why not make yourself the hero of your story?

Thursday 23rd

All of a sudden, you will have a new idea regarding the organisation of your home environment. Your priority is for neatness, but what if you could include some comfort too? Take the time to follow up on your ideas right away, so that they don't slip away.

Friday 24th

Reality versus fantasy. Why should there even have to be a choice? You don't have to pick one over the other if you decide to watch a fantastical film at home. Make drinks and snacks that fit the theme of your movie to further blur the boundary between fact and fiction.

Saturday 25th

You may still be feeling inspired by the recent reality versus fantasy theme. If you are, you could become even more creative with it. Why not develop a fantastical story of your own, and then throw a party where you can act it out for your friends?

Sunday 26th

Love yourself, and love yourself some more. This can be your motto today if you feel any doubts rising up. Be compassionate with yourself, and push those doubts away. You cannot focus on love and fear at the same time. Choose love, and you will be sure to go far.

Monday 27th

The focus shifts to health and habits today. Have you made any changes lately to improve your health? If you haven't, now is the time to do so. Taking better care of yourself is the ultimate way to put your recently improved self-love skills into action.

Tuesday 28th

Today has a magical vibe to it, and all is harmonious. You want to expand your horizons, ideals and dreams as well as the impact you have. You can use this wonderful energy to do some volunteering work, which will in turn support your need to serve the world.

Wednesday 29th

Venus is finally leaving her shadow, which means she will be covering new territory from now on. Your transformation is complete! Look in the mirror and fully appreciate all that you have been through, and all of the changes you have made. You are now a butterfly.

Thursday 3oth

Your mind connects to the unconscious today, and
Jupiter comes into the mix by expanding your horizons.
Be compassionate about anything you discover hidden
in your subconscious, and just observe it for now. You
will know what to do next in a few days, but until then
try not to fall into any old behaviours.

Friday 31st

The Moon is back in Capricorn, giving you the chance
to assess the ground and structure you recently created.
Can it carry your weight or do you feel it should be
transformed once again? A trust issue could come up in
your neighbourhood. How do you want to respond?

AUGUST
·················

Saturday 1st
Your mind is again pondering your desires and needs.
You are not only pondering these mentally, but
emotionally too. You are especially keen to find ways to
combine your desires and needs with your new sense
of self-worth and self-love. If you can find the right mix,
others may just take the cue and mirror your behaviour.

Sunday 2nd
You will want to explore the unknown today, such as
a foreign language or country that you are yet to visit.
Maybe you want to do some research or pick up a
guidebook. Expect to find the unexpected. Who knows
where you will end up?

Monday 3rd
The importance of exploration will be highlighted for
you this month, and today you are likely to make some
travel plans. The place, or places, you choose to visit will
have a major influence on your life in the upcoming
years. Stay curious about how this will all unfold.

Tuesday 4th

You will be faced with some tough questions today. They concern the foundation, structures and grounding that are necessary to increase your levels of intimacy and trust. You will soon move on to another topic, so ponder this area thoughtfully while you can. Don't miss this opportunity, it will be valuable.

Wednesday 5th

It is now time to focus on the creative expression of your thoughts. You can do this through writing, for yourself or for others, vlogging, or perhaps through a podcast or your own play. There are many options available, both for personal satisfaction or public consumption. Which one you want to choose?

Thursday 6th

Venus is finally moving to the north node. This aligns your sense of beauty, love and harmony with the overall theme of self-realisation. It is a huge and well-deserved development that will be visible in your renewed self-confidence. Celebrate yourself today, and buy something to underline your true beauty.

Friday 7th

You will want to spend this day with one of your social groups, where you can continue to work on a project. Be aware that tension could arise. One part of the group wants a very direct approach, whilst the other part wants to play safe and avoid risk. You will be able to find a solution, whilst acknowledging and soothing the feelings of both sides.

Saturday 8th

Your emotions will align beautifully with your thoughts, which is almost like a guarantee for a great day. You will be able to put lots of energy into your creative endeavours, be it on your own or on a project with others. Happy creating!

Sunday 9th

Are you ready to deal with a little more tension, just for today? Once again, the theme of trust and intimacy arises, and you may want to reassure a friend or loved one that their secrets are safe with you. You will want to receive the same promise in return.

Monday 10th

It's time to rest and relax. You will now want to enjoy the summer sun, so why not arrange to see friends at the park or organise a trip to the beach? However, make sure that you also reserve some time for yourself.

Tuesday 11th

Your mind and emotions are not aligned today. While you want to step back emotionally, you also want to express mentally. However, you cannot always separate the head and heart. Try your best to bring them both together. Try writing in your journal, or calling your best friend.

Wednesday 12th

Today, you no longer feel the need to retreat from the world, and are happy and willing to be out and about. Be sure to explore all of the supportive energy on offer. If you've been invited to a summer barbecue, go. If not, organise one of your own.

Thursday 13th

Indecision might be today's keyword, as you don't really know how you want to act in your community and social groups. This puts you in a kind of conflict with yourself. It is okay to be unsure, even if it feels scary sometimes. Don't act today.

Friday 14th

You are still weighing up all your options, but it might be best to discuss the issues openly. You will not only be able to clearly hear your own thoughts by talking about them, but also those of everyone involved. This will help you to find a solution that serves all.

Saturday 15th

Today's energy puts you in a very good place. You will finally realise what you want to act upon creatively, and will be highly influenced by your dreams. You will be able to combine logic and fantasy in an amazing way, and may end up creating a story that inspires others to engage more with their dreams.

Sunday 16th

Today's energy is a little edgy, and you might not want to step out of your comfort zone. Actually, there is nothing you can do about it, so make it easier by accepting it. Dare to act the way you want to, and not the way demanded of you.

Monday 17th

It is quite possible that you will have the urge to continue with your creative work. This could manifest in different ways. It could be through planning a street party in your neighbourhood, or through organising a barbecue to celebrate the latest sports event. Just make sure you give it a personal note.

Tuesday 18th

Happy Leo New Moon! This lunar cycle is all about your creativity and immediate surroundings, such as your neighbourhood, or the people and animals you live alongside. Try to remain present when you interact, and use your imagination to create something that will beautify your life.

Wednesday 19th

The Moon is now entering Virgo, so you will become more emotionally involved with your home life. What does home mean to you, and where do you feel most at home in yourself? Whatever your answers, just be sure to consider your emotions first.

Thursday 20th

After yesterday's emotional soul-searching about your home life, Mercury enters that area to request a more logical approach. However, be aware that you should value both your emotions and your thoughts. The mind should never be allowed to outrank the emotions.

Friday 21st

The Moon in Libra means it is time to create harmony and balance in your life. Where have you been off-kilter lately, and what do you need to do in order to maintain balance again? Use this time to find or create a solution that is both fair and just.

Saturday 22nd

The Sun enters Virgo today and that means your focus will shift to home, family and ancestors for the next thirty days. This is all about roots. If you have strong roots, you can bend with the wind. What comes to mind if you think about family and ancestors? Do you want to dive into your family's history?

Sunday 23rd

Your to-do list is most likely to be occupying you on this hopefully sunny Sunday. It might not be the most exciting thing to do, but it is useful. Take your mind off of any potentially boring tasks by talking on the phone with friends or family at the same time.

Monday 24th

Today is a little tricky, so the main advice is to stay calm. You might come into conflict with a person of authority, possibly a boss, police officer or judge, and could react very emotionally. Try to take a deep breath and count to ten.

Tuesday 25th

The energy is beautiful once more. It is a great day to surprise a loved one with a treat. Take them out to dinner, or book a spa session. Ideally, you should choose somewhere you can both talk and open up. Be prepared to connect on a deeper level.

Wednesday 26th

You are still focussing on your relationships today, whilst now also trying to balance your own interests. This challenge is an ongoing lesson for you, but you need to be true to yourself and stay conscious of your needs and desires.

Thursday 27th

Somebody should invent a magical Thursday, as today's energy could be just that. If you dare to act in your best interests, and by valuing yourself as well as your partner, you will get to see just how your dream life could become real.

Friday 28th

Some unexpected emotions arise in you today, but they are easy and happy ones. Isn't it funny to see what feelings are hidden beneath the surface? When such feelings finally rise up they often contain rich treasures. Embrace your emotions today and be surprised by what they bring.

Saturday 29th

This is a busy day, and you will barely have a minute to rest. The energy is quite a mixed bag, so you may encounter fun and easy situations as well as difficult ones. If you can remain flexible, you will manage to have an exciting day.

Sunday 30th

Today, you will be trying to find the balance between luxury and resources. It is not always fun to think and talk about money, but it is necessary to do so. Once you have looked over your finances, you will have a greater clarity and be able to act accordingly.

Monday 31st

You will end the month feeling positive. It is possible that you will start to plan the route or even book the flight or accommodation for the big trip you have been dreaming of. If you are travelling with friends, you will easily be able to accommodate everyone's needs.

SEPTEMBER

....

Tuesday 1st

Your mental energy is high today and you not only think fast, but also act fast. This is especially true of anything in your home and family life. You will also find a solution to a problem regarding money, taxes or inheritance that you have been pondering for a while.

Wednesday 2nd

Happy Full Moon in Pisces! This Full Moon highlights your career and legacy. It also promises a helpful surprise. This may manifest itself as a family member supporting your next career steps, helping you to build a solid foundation for success.

Thursday 3rd

Today gives you the opportunity to think about ways to handle your responsibilities, and you can expect this to happen with your friends. They may help you to work out the tasks and jobs you actually want to take on, and those that don't excite you any more.

Friday 4th

You will be in two minds today. Part of you wants to stay home, and tackle the housework or create a rota for chores. The other side of you wants to get out and see some friends. It is completely possible to do both, you will just need a plan of action.

Saturday 5th

Your planetary guide Mercury comes into the sign of Libra, and this means you will want to connect even more with others, and also express yourself creatively in many ways. You should definitely make time to meet with friends and have fun together during the next few weeks.

Sunday 6th

Are you ready and willing to treat yourself? It does not need to be expensive, but choose something that you love. It could be something you don't regularly indulge in, like a slice of cake from a special cafe or a bouquet of your favourite flowers.

Monday 7th

This may be a day of surprising emotions, but also one of optimistic vibes. Just enjoy yourself to the fullest, and try not to let your emotions lead you astray. The surprise most likely concerns yourself and a hidden motive, but it will pass quickly.

Tuesday 8th

This is a busy day, but fortunately all the action is happening in a harmonious way. In fact, this is just the sort of day you enjoy most. A loved one or friend that is very dear to you may have an issue they need help with, and you will help them to find a fantastic solution.

Wednesday 9th

Sun Jupiter days are the best, and this one is no exception. Joy and excitement will fill the air as you become able to increase the trust and intimacy you feel at home and with your family. You might want to tell your best friend the good news right away.

Thursday 10th

Mars goes retrograde in his own sign of Aries. This means there are changes on the horizon regarding the groups and communities you are involved in, and even your friendships. Who will stay in your life, who will leave and who will eventually enter? All this will soon be determined.

Friday 11th

This Friday, you might not even want to go to work. You may have a tendency to dive away into fantasy in order to escape the real world. Actually, if your schedule allows that, do it. Just remember that you will need to take care of business another time.

Saturday 12th

Now comes the time to get on with the jobs you put off doing yesterday. You will be proud of what you accomplish as the day progresses, and you could be unexpectedly rewarded with a surprise. It is the type of surprise that will really put a smile on your face.

Sunday 13th

Jupiter, the planet of buoyancy and expansion, is moving direct, and this time he is finishing the story about deepening your intimacy and bringing fortune to your bank account. Just wait and see what treasure he will bring you during the next month.

Monday 14th

It is a transformative day that asks you to speak up. Not by telling rumours or stories, but instead by revealing your true identity. This will most likely have something to do with your home life and family issues. If you dare to show your true face, it will certainly pay off.

Tuesday 15th

Today's energy is very interesting. You will seek to express yourself to the outside world, but there is still a part of you that you are holding back because you are worried it is not beautiful enough. Everyone is perfect and unique, and so are you.

Wednesday 16th

Today is likely to be quiet, and you could even feel tired. This is because the energy is drawing back ahead of the New Moon. Take it easy today, and allow yourself to rest should you become unusually tired. A little nap can work wonders.

Thursday 17th

The New Moon in Virgo brings you the chance to look again at your home, family and ancestors. Whether you start to create a family tree or look at old photographs, all sorts of investigation can lead you to something of value and importance. Even questioning your parents could be the route to take.

Friday 18th

Are you emotionally ready for expansion? The Sun is in a happy conversation with Saturn, allowing you to consolidate your structure. This structure will allow you to move forwards, and could certainly mean that you receive some money from an authority figure.

Saturday 19th

Today is a little edgy, as you really want to interact with others, but tensions are arising. You may wonder whether you can really trust your friends, and you may feel as though you have no clue if they are real and true to you.

Sunday 20th

Somehow the energy is wonky today, but, and this is the good news, only for a short moment. The rest of the day will be quiet, and you will be able to start your next attempt at a healthier diet or exercise regime. Why not try a green smoothie?

Monday 21st

Your relationships will fall under the spotlight, and you will try to wrap your head around the idea of intimacy. You may be questioning why it feels so difficult. The answer could be that you are having a hard time committing. It doesn't mean you are unable to, but it must be to the right person.

Tuesday 22nd

The Sun is entering your fifth house of joy, creation, passion and children, so you can expect an interesting and happy month. Mentally, you receive the next important puzzle piece regarding what you should hold on to in the future, and what you should let go of from the past.

Wednesday 23rd

Your mind is in conflict with your responsibilities. There is something bothering you, not just a bit but a lot. Ponder how you could approach the situation differently, and what solutions are available to you. You won't decide today, so there is no need for action. Just stay observant and don't snub anybody.

Thursday 24th

You are finally ready to take action. However, will you
actually go through with your plans, or will you stumble?
Your emotions will take you on the wildest of rides today,
so you would be wise to tread decisively yet carefully.

Friday 25th

Things will become clearer today, as you emotionally
consider the transformation, structure and expansion
inherent in your resources. As the day goes on, you will
notice that everything fits perfectly. The highest roads
will open up to you as you move forwards.

Saturday 26th

Having spent so much time pondering difficult topics
lately, you will be in the mood for a weekend of fun and
adventure. If you are going away, pack your suitcase or
bag lightly. You should leave space for bringing home a
momentum or two of your trip.

Sunday 27th

This weekend is shaping up to be one about exploration,
and today you will start to think about your overall
health and fitness. Try to be as objective as possible
when you assess the changes that need to be made. For
now, just consider the options. The time to implement
them will be later.

Monday 28th

A dreamy Monday awaits you. However, this might not be the type of energy that makes you work the hardest. You may start to dream of a new career path that allows you to have more time with your loved ones. It is never too late to make dreams come true.

Tuesday 29th

Saturn is moving direct again, which also marks a milestone in your journey. You have been considering many shifts, changes and serious subjects lately, but you can now move forwards. What is coming up next will be much more exciting, and there are only a few more weeks to wait until the real shift starts to happen.

Wednesday 30th

Whereas before you were considering the very foundations of a relationship, you will now want to look at the actions needed to sustain them. You must try to find a way that does not compromise your integrity, whilst also showing faith in your partner. You must let your guard down if you are to develop your newly found trust.

OCTOBER

....

Thursday 1st

Today's Full Moon in Aries is an extra powerful one,
as it coincides with Mars retrograde. This will shine
the spotlight on your social groups and communities.
Conflicts may also be highlighted, but just for the
purpose of resolving them. If you can agree to disagree,
all will be fine.

Friday 2nd

The time has come to beautify your home and family
life. This could range from total refurbishment to
redecoration, or to improving family relations. Whatever
you make this about, strive to achieve the perfect
balance of form and function for the best results.

Saturday 3rd

Some me-time is in order. You will be in the mood
for solitude and the chance to sit quietly with your
thoughts. As you relax, you may start to consider what
you need in your home to feel happy, safe and nurtured.
You may even feel inspired to make changes right away.

Sunday 4th

There could be a tendency to hide away today. As you try to align your heart and mind, you might be surprised by the effort it would take to leave your comfort zone. Are you willing to at least try? You may prefer to ponder it a little longer.

Monday 5th

With your recent transformation having taken place, Pluto is getting ready to set you free of any further investigations. He will still continue to linger in this space, but you will feel that your evolution and development are now much more defined.

Tuesday 6th

The Gemini Moon puts the focus squarely on you. Or should that be you two, owing to your dualistic nature? You will enjoy posing questions about yourself, but it will be even more fun to discuss those questions with others. There are two sides to every coin, after all.

Wednesday 7th

Here it is, the liberating thought that offers you freedom. You will need to balance it with your day-to-day routine, but it will make for fascinating thinking. Your main task is to write it down and consider it more deeply.

Thursday 8th

Receiving is today's keyword. What are you allowing yourself to receive? Do you let someone else care for you or do you prefer to nurture yourself? This may also relate to how you look after your physical body, as well as your diet and exercise regime. How can you improve your routines?

Friday 9th

Today's energy might feel intense. You may want to act impulsively when presented with a question about power, but ask yourself if it is really worth it. Would you benefit from taking a big breath and counting to ten before responding?

Saturday 10th

A sudden event may change your perspective completely. You are currently considering improving your home and family life, and today could bring new insight. You may now decide to move home completely, or want to rethink an entire decoration scheme. Talk it through before you act.

Sunday 11th

You want to bring balance and harmony to your closest relationship, and this may ironically be best achieved through conflict. The difference of opinion may be about childcare or housework, but airing these grievances will help you and your significant other to resolve them, and strengthen your bond.

Monday 12th

Do you need more encouragement to express yourself? Have you completed any writing projects? You may have had so many new ideas that were unable to finish a single one. However you respond to these questions, doesn't really matter. Write, talk and express yourself today.

Tuesday 13th

Today is a big test. A test of your friends and social groups. It is a time to take action, and this may involve leaving people behind that no longer interest you. You will be looking for new and exciting friends who pique your interest to fill the void.

Wednesday 14th

Another Mercury retrograde is ahead. This time, your planetary ruler is moving backwards through Scorpio. This gives you plenty of time to now re-evaluate your health, habits and day-to-day routines. You will reach interesting conclusions if you are prepared to dive deep.

Thursday 15th

Intensity ahead! You are trying to solve the tension between harmony, fairness and manipulation. It is one thing to give freely, but quite another thing entirely to give in order to receive. You need to be very honest with yourself. Are you giving to give or are you giving to receive?

Friday 16th

Happy New Moon in Libra! This New Moon is all about your joys and passions, and the way you express them creatively and with others. If there are children in your life, spend some quality time with them today. You may be deeply inspired by their enthusiasm and curiosity.

Saturday 17th

As the Moon enters your sixth house, you will return to your day-to-day routines. With the Moon crossing over retrograde Mercury, it is possible that you will have the first real insight into what habits you want to change and why. There may even be a habit you were completely unaware of until now.

Sunday 18th

Today asks for you to become aware of the relationship between your passions and your responsibilities. Is there a way to change some habits so that they can allow for more joy while you fulfil your responsibilities? It doesn't have to be one or the other.

Monday 19th

Relationships are a theme today, and, on the one hand, there are beautiful developments happening in your home and family life. At the same time, however, something feels amiss regarding your friends and social groups. It is not easy to cover all bases, even for a Geminian like you.

Tuesday 20th

You may have a sudden insight today into a habit you wish to break. It is possibly something you have been doing for the sole purpose of appeasing others, rather than because it suits you. What would serve your own needs much better?

Wednesday 21st

You have been making such fantastic progress lately in trusting others, and the day will be drenched in loving connections as a result. This is likely to be with your family, or possibly someone you refer to as family, such as a dear friend or pet. Enjoy this time.

Thursday 22nd

As the Sun enters Scorpio, the emphasis is put on adjusting your health and nutrition, as well as your day-to-day routines. The next thirty days will help you to implement all the things you been thinking about since Mercury moved into this sign.

Friday 23rd

The Moon is in Aquarius, and you will likely feel some wanderlust. You know that a trip away will be great for your family, but will it be detrimental to all the changes you are about to make with your health? Will you be able to resist the urge to indulge if you go on holiday?

Saturday 24th

You sometimes have a hard time making long-term commitments in your personal life. Yet you actually can today, and will do so from the heart. As you make your promises, you will be relieved to find that you do not feel pushed or trapped in any way. This is progress.

Sunday 25th

Today is Mercury Cazimi, which means your planetary guide will meet with the Sun. You will be able to merge all your preliminary thoughts with your current reality, and there will be a shift towards a more embodied experience. All of this will prove very useful for helping you to implement change.

Monday 26th

The week begins on a happy note, as your emotions align with your entire being. This day promises some excitement, which suits your mood. Not everyone around you will be feeling quite as upbeat, however, so why not be the person to light up the day?

Tuesday 27th

As the Moon crosses Neptune, you are likely to be restless and easily distracted. You will do your best to focus, but it might be wiser to admit defeat and work a shorter day. Once back at home, try to occupy yourself with a favourite hobby until the mood passes.

Wednesday 28th

You will feel driven to find a balance today. You may be tempted to dig your heels in on a matter, but that would certainly not support your need for harmony. Instead, take a step back from your emotions to explore what is behind them. This is the best way for you to achieve the balance you crave.

Thursday 29th

Your friends may hit a nerve today. You are unlikely to tell them about it, and may begin a difficult dialogue with yourself instead. Don't judge or blame yourself. You are having a human experience, and everybody has something they are sensitive about. Your task is just to be aware of it.

Friday 30th

Today may start awkwardly, as there could be some tension in the air. This is not necessarily bad, however, as you are likely to find a creative solution hidden within conflict. As the day progresses, the energy will ease. Allow yourself some much-needed me-time.

Saturday 31st

Happy Halloween! This year, Halloween is tied to a very powerful Full Moon in Taurus. Whatever your plans are today, they are likely to turn out very differently. Trick or treat? You just don't know what you're going to get.

NOVEMBER

· · · · · · · · · · · · · · · · · ·

Sunday 1st
November is here, and it brings with it a spirit
of revelation. As the Moon is enjoying a smooth
conversation with Jupiter, you should expect a happy
surprise. You may receive a windfall, or it might be that
you find a treasure you thought you had lost.

Monday 2nd
You start the day in a quiet mood, but with an inner
stability and peace. The pace will soon start to pick
up speed, and you will have many good talks and
connections. If you can remain in a grounded mood, the
day will indeed be rich.

Tuesday 3rd
You will finally be able to combine your joys and passions
with the communities and groups you are engaging
with. It is possible you may join a brand-new group that
feels more in sync with your personality and values.
Alternatively, you may start to express yourself more in an
existing group, so that your experience deepens.

Wednesday 4th

Congratulations, you have made it through the final
Mercury retrograde of the year. Today may bring a
glimpse of where the future is leading you. Is it where
you are hoping to go? Are you ready and prepared for
it? Do you need to make any changes first?

Thursday 5th

You might be tempted to spend a lot of money today,
particularly on something that would bring you comfort.
It could be a cashmere blanket or silk sheets. However,
it is quite possible that you will have changed your mind
by tomorrow. Save your cash and sleep on it.

Friday 6th

Money issues may come up today, as it is possible that
you will not want to invest as much in your social groups
as they demand. Take a closer look at what they are
asking. Is it really too much? What value does it have
that money can't buy?

Saturday 7th

Usually, you enjoy an amazing energy whenever the
Moon shifts into Leo. You feel inspired and are willing to
communicate and connect on your highest level. Today
is no different, and you will love all the ideas that are
flying around. Try to write down the best ones, at least.

Sunday 8th

The Moon is still in Leo, but now faces tension from the Sun. This may manifest as a lesson about the importance of taking care of yourself. You can only cope with being busy if you give your body something it can work with. Why not cook a meal with friends to relax?

Monday 9th

Your focus will turn to home and family today, and you will probably be trying to make time for the children in your life. It might be that you need to take one of your own children along on errands, or you want to start a new tradition or hobby with a niece or nephew.

Tuesday 10th

Mercury is about to enter Scorpio, and has collected all sorts of ideas about balancing your day-to-day routines. The universe is urging you to think deeply about your health and habits, and wants to help set you up in a new way.

Wednesday 11th

This is a good day to have one-to-one conversations. You will probably not go out and will stay at home instead, which will allow you to go deep into devotion with that special someone. This can be a day of bonding, bliss and tenderness.

Thursday 12th

There it is, the final meeting of Jupiter and Pluto. They won't meet again for over a decade. Together, they are trying to combine your highest and lowest needs and desires to set you up for further expansion and growth. You have made tremendous shifts so far, and this marks another starting point of a new attitude.

Friday 13th

You still need to catch up to your new attitude emotionally, and that is what you will be trying to do today. There is a sense of edginess, but this will pass by soon. You can actually soften the edges by doing something good for your body, or by taking care of your home.

Saturday 14th

Mars retrograde is over. You have had to re-evaluate your own behaviour and that of others in your social groups. Mars will continue to highlight this area, even at the start of 2021. For now, you can focus on engaging with your friends, as there are only little adjustments to be made.

Sunday 15th

The New Moon in Scorpio offers you the opportunity to make the necessary shifts and adjustments regarding your health and fitness. This topic has come up quite a lot recently, and now is the perfect time to make some resolutions, create a plan and stick to it.

Monday 16th

You are so creative, but are you also willing to put in the work needed to shine as bright and big as you can? Sometimes, you need to stick with something in order to gain influence or even be recognised. With today's energy, you can make it happen – if it is something that really makes your heart sing.

Tuesday 17th

Mercury and Uranus have been arguing a lot lately and they are coming back together for another round. There is a chance it will be very inspiring, or will allow you to show your rebellious nature. You could surprise others as much as you could surprise yourself.

Wednesday 18th

You could struggle with an issue in your social groups today. Your friends may ask you to commit to something, but you will feel a strong resistance from within. Do you really want to stick with that resistance or do you want to become involved more deeply?

Thursday 19th

The Sun is in a very positive flow to Saturn, helping you to pour self-discipline into any new healthy habits. It could be something as simple as a regular walk outside, but it hopefully involves changes to your diet. Even small adjustments can go a long way.

Friday 20th

Your emotions are in conflict with your mental energy, and you are still trying to weigh up the pros and cons of creating routine versus your sense of adventure. It does not need to be so difficult. Try to think of smaller routines that are easy to implement wherever you may be.

Saturday 21st

The Sun moves into Sagittarius, highlighting your relationships. You should expect some important developments now. Elsewhere, Venus, the goddess of love, moves into Scorpio, where she is able to bring beauty to the health habits you have been working on lately.

Sunday 22nd

It is understandable if you find today's energy too fast-paced. There are two planets at the very first degree, so you are probably just adjusting to the change. Luckily, it is Sunday so you can take it easy. Dive into daydreams, movies and fantasies.

Monday 23rd

The dreamy vibe continues on this Monday. You will probably be surrounded by many people, when all you want to do is just be with your loved ones. However, this would be a great day to go to a concert, play or the ballet. This would support all the energies.

Tuesday 24th

There is a sense of healing in the air today. As you start to implement your new habits, you will finally see how they can help you to draw boundaries with others. This is especially true for the social groups and friends you are interacting with.

Wednesday 25th

You will have lots of energy available to you today. It is as if you could go non-stop from meeting to meeting, and then still have the energy to take your loved one out to dinner in the evening. As long as you feel your energy is high, just enjoy it.

Thursday 26th

Impatience could be today's keyword. Things may not happen as quickly as you want them to, and you may be prone to overreacting. If you do, people around you will certainly notice. You should be careful to hold your tongue, as you won't be able to take back those words once they are out.

Friday 27th

Sometimes, you become stubborn and resistant to change. It is an inner resistance that does not serve you. You will be able to beautify and harmonise yourself and your life if you can let that resistance go. Once you do, you'll see how much you will profit from the change.

Saturday 28th

Saturday starts with a nice, easy energy, and you can expect a wonderfully quiet weekend. This is a great time for wellness, comforting food and relaxation. If you can also be with a loved one, you'll probably like it even more. Use this time to recharge if you are on your own.

Sunday 29th

The easy and relaxing vibe continues, and you could include meditation in your schedule. There are many forms of meditation that would serve this purpose, such as t'ai chi or qigong. Whichever you choose, enjoy the chance to settle your ever-flowing mind.

Monday 30th

The month ends with a powerhouse of a Full Moon: a partial lunar eclipse in Gemini. It illuminates the work you have done so far with your self-realisation, and sets a milestone. Be grateful and appreciative for what you have already changed and received, but stay mindful that there is more to come.

DECEMBER

....

Tuesday 1st

As you enter this final month of 2020, Mercury, your planetary guide, enters your relationship area. This adds to the importance of relationships in your life, and you will be thinking about them a lot. This process will be prove to be vital, but remember to include your feelings and intuition in your contemplation.

Wednesday 2nd

You should try to take good care of yourself today, and find a way to include your body in your sensual experience. Sometimes your mind is running here, there and everywhere, and your body is left behind. Try to be in the moment as best as you can, by focusing on your physical senses.

Thursday 3rd

Physical activity could be a good outlet for today's tension, and will certainly help to avoid arguments. This could be through swimming, dancing, skiing or perhaps hiking. Treat your body well, and enjoy the energy running through your veins. It is a great day to feel alive.

Friday 4th

The day may start a little uneasily as you will have to deal with responsibilities early on. Once the working day ends, however, a happy and joyful vibe will emerge. Your mind and emotions will be fully in sync, and you will be ready to have some fun. This could be an after-work party or a get-together in your neighbourhood. Enjoy it – it is a reward for your hard work today.

Saturday 5th

The weekend starts with a surprise, perhaps with someone saying something that intimidates you. Don't stick with this feeling for too long though, and take action instead. This could be by talking to that person openly, allowing you the chance to speak your truth and heal the situation. There is nothing to gain from inaction, only regrets.

Sunday 6th

Christmas is on its way, so you will most likely be having fun buying gifts or hanging decorations today. If a family member comments that it is too early to feel festive, smile and carry on as you were. This is a wonderful time of the year to express yourself and your creativity, embrace it and enjoy yourself. 'Tis the season!

Monday 7th

Once your Christmas decorations are up, you may want to turn your hand to baking. You will enjoy cooking on your own, but may later want to share the results with your family members. Why don't you try adding a new twist to old favourites?

Tuesday 8th

It is an amazing day to get prep work done, as you will be able to focus fully on tasks. The next few weeks will be very busy, so you will thank yourself later for getting ahead of time and doing the groundwork in advance for the coming days. If the phone rings, you may want to just screen your calls and concentrate on your to-do list instead. Try not to get distracted!

Wednesday 9th

There might be a little dissonance between your relationship and business obligations. You should take care of business, but it should not keep you away from your loved ones for too long. Maybe you can bring a little fun into the mix? This will be easy if you let your inner child out to play.

Thursday 10th

The focus returns to healthy habits and the transformation you have been working on recently. You might not be able to see how it will all play out exactly because there is a foggy energy, but you will know on a deeper level what it takes. You can do this.

Friday 11th

This day marks a major release point. You will be able
to actively let go of a habit or belief that has been
restricting your relationship experience. With this, you
can create space for new, healthier ways of relating that
will be totally in alignment with your values and identity.

Saturday 12th

The energy of letting go actively is still very present
today, so you may want to get clear about it and maybe
do a symbolic act. For example, you could try writing
down all the old beliefs and habits on a piece of paper,
before shredding or burying it.

Sunday 13th

The Moon joins the Sun and Mercury in Sagittarius,
so you are now also emotionally in the space of your
relationship realm. It would be a great day to spend with
your beloved or somebody dear to you. It would be best
to do something exciting together, as this experience will
tighten your bond. Be bold and have fun!

Monday 14th

As the year draws to a close, the universe begins
bringing in big energies again. Today's New Moon is
conjunct the south node, so it is asking you to take the
essence and gifts of your past relationship experiences
and let go of everything else. Start to seed something
new here instead.

Tuesday 15th

Venus, the goddess of love, joins the planets already in Sagittarius, highlighting your relationships. You are now ready to take further action regarding your beliefs about friendship, and love in general. It will become easier for you to understand how your perception is affecting your experiences.

Wednesday 16th

The energy today is transformative, and you may find yourself wanting to break free of all boundaries and limitations. However, what if the structures you are operating in are not as limiting as you think? What if you could actually use them to your advantage?

Thursday 17th

You might think that Christmas is the next big event, but it is actually Saturn's departure from his home sign of Capricorn. He is also leaving behind your area of intimacy, trust and shared resources, having completed work on your new foundation of trust.

Friday 18th

It's another big day, as Mercury has one last meeting with the Sun before the year ends. This always offers a chance to reset, and to align your mind with your entire being. This time, it could also offer the opportunity to align with your new attitude towards relationships.

Saturday 19th

One big event is following the next at the moment.
Today is the final day of Jupiter in Capricorn. Jupiter
spends about a year in each sign, and during 2020 he
wanted to give you a new sense of abundance, while also
increasing your trust and intimacy levels. Has he taught
you a few lessons?

Sunday 20th

Today is very significant. Jupiter enters Aquarius and
meets there with Saturn. When these two giants come
together, it marks the start of a completely new cycle.
Their work in Aquarius will lay a foundation that Pluto
can work with once he arrives in 2024.

Monday 21st

Happy winter solstice! Today marks the shortest day and
longest night of the year. In ancient times, people used
to stay up and watch the sunrise. This day also marks
the ingress of Sun into Capricorn, which means your
area of intimacy, trust, power and shared resources is
highlighted furthermore.

Tuesday 22nd

Today could be busy, and you may want to work out
what action you should take next. Try not to become
stressed, even if you have a long list of tasks ahead of
you. Try to move forwards as directly as possible, and
tackle the tasks that are most important.

Wednesday 23rd

Unfortunately, today could be as stressful as yesterday. Any tasks you were able to complete may need to be looked at again or changed. You will understandably feel frustrated, but it is important to keep a cool head. Press pause and create a plan before proceeding.

Thursday 24th

If possible, it would be good to take a break today. Thoughts and worries about money and gifts may be troubling you. Don't be so hard on yourself. Christmas is all about love, and as long as you remember that everything will be fine.

Friday 25th

Merry Christmas! May the surprises you receive be jolly and bright. May love light up your heart, and may conversations be inspiring and loving. May all that you give be well received, and may the connections between all the people around you be strong.

Saturday 26th

Can you believe you are in the final week of the year? Today is wonderful to dive into Christmas stories that highlight love, and to just have a relaxing day. Think amazing food, probably with a hint of luxury, and the satisfied silence that will follow.

Sunday 27th

Today you want to get out, see other people, play board games, share the latest news and events and just be in your element. Do all of that. However, as much as everyone may enjoy your entertainment skills, remember to listen to their stories too.

Monday 28th

Emotionally, you will align with your future purpose, self-worth and self-realisation today. The Sun is also in an amazing aspect to Uranus, so you could feel a liberating sense of freedom that may foreshadow the future. The energy is high and you will probably be busy all day.

Tuesday 29th

The last Full Moon in 2020 arrives, and it is in Cancer. This highlights all the progress you have made regarding nurturing yourself, how you handle money and what you consider to be of value. You have put a lot of effort into this area, and can now finally see the first results blossoming.

Wednesday 30th

Venus will ask you today how you can bring a higher
level of love into your main relationship. How can you
strengthen your bond, but also widen the horizons? The
relationship you desire combines adventure, exploration
and the deepest kind of love you can imagine. If you can
dream it, you can make it happen.

Thursday 31st

It's the final day of 2020. As you get ready to celebrate,
take time to reflect on the tests, transformations and gifts
this year has brought you. What was the most challenging
event? What was the biggest surprise? Who was most
important to you? Let gratitude lead you into 2021.

Gemini

....

PEOPLE WHO
SHARE YOUR SIGN

PEOPLE WHO
SHARE YOUR SIGN

· · · · · · · · · · · · · · · · · ·

The voices of Geminians are loud, clear and capable of moving mountains. Their influential and contagious words often have a global impact, whether it's a Tweet from U.S. President Donald Trump or a song from Bob Dylan. Discover the articulate Geminians who share your exact birthday and see if you can spot the similarities.

May 22nd

Novak Djokovic (1987), Arturo Vidal (1987), Maggie Q (1979), Ginnifer Goodwin (1978), Naomi Campbell (1970), Steven Morrissey (1959), George Best (1946), Laurence Olivier (1907)

May 23rd

Ryan Coogler (1986), Manuela Schwesig (1974), George Osborne (1971), Melissa McBride (1965), Drew Carey (1958), Marvelous Marvin Hagler (1954), Joan Collins (1933), Rosemary Clooney (1928)

May 24th

Joey Logano (1990), G-Eazy (1989), Dermot O'Leary (1973), Eric Cantona (1966), Rajdeep Sardesai (1965), Kristin Scott Thomas (1960), Priscilla Presley (1945), Patti LaBelle (1944), Bob Dylan (1941), Queen Victoria (1819)

May 25th

Brec Bassinger (1999), Aly Raisman (1994), Roman Reigns (1985), Rasheeda (1982), Joe King (1980), Cillian Murphy (1976), Mike Myers (1963), Paul Weller (1958), Ian McKellen (1939)

May 26th

Juan Cuadrado (1988), Scott Disick (1983), Lauryn Hill (1975), Helena Bonham Carter (1966), Lenny Kravitz (1964), Jeremy Corbyn (1949), Stevie Nicks (1948), John Wayne (1907)

May 27th

Lily-Rose Depp (1999), André 3000 (1975), Jamie Oliver (1975), Paul Bettany (1971), Joseph Fiennes (1970), Paul Gascoigne (1967), Heston Blumenthal (1966), Henry Kissinger (1923), Christopher Lee (1922)

May 28th

Cameron Boyce (1999), John Stones (1994), Carey Mulligan (1985), Jake Johnson (1978), Kylie Minogue (1968), John Fogerty (1945), Rudy Giuliani (1944), Gladys Knight (1944)

May 29th

Maika Monroe (1993), Riley Keough (1989), Melanie B (1975), Laverne Cox (1972), Noel Gallagher (1967), Carol Kirkwood (1962), La Toya Jackson (1956), U.S President John F. Kennedy (1917)

May 30th

Sean Giambrone (1999), Jake Short (1997), Jennifer
Ellison (1983), Steven Gerrard (1980), Remy Ma (1980),
Cee Lo Green (1975), Idina Menzel (1971),
Mark Sheppard (1964)

May 31st

Normani (1996), Azealia Banks (1991), Reggie Yates (1983),
Colin Farrell (1976), Brooke Shields (1965), Viktor Orbán
(1963), Lea Thompson (1961), Clint Eastwood (1930), Walt
Whitman (1819)

June 1st

Tom Holland (1996), Amy Schumer (1981), Alanis
Morissette (1974), Heidi Klum (1973), Archie Panjabi
(1972), Ronnie Wood (1947), Morgan Freeman (1937),
Marilyn Monroe (1926)

June 2nd

Sergio Agüero (1988), Morena Baccarin (1979), Dominic
Cooper (1978), Justin Long (1978), Zachary Quinto (1977),
A.J. Styles (1977), Wentworth Miller (1972), Andy Cohen
(1968), Jeanine Pirro (1951)

June 3rd

Mario Götze (1992), Imogen Poots (1989), Michelle Keegan (1987), Rafael Nadal (1986), Anderson Cooper (1967), James Purefoy (1964), Susannah Constantine (1962), Allen Ginsberg (1926), Tony Curtis (1925), M. Karunanidhi (1924), George V, King of England (1865)

June 4th

Mackenzie Ziegler (2004), Lucky Blue Smith (1998), Brandon Jenner (1981), T.J. Miller (1981), Russell Brand (1975), Angelina Jolie (1975), Izabella Scorupco (1970)

June 5th

Troye Sivan (1995), Amanda Crew (1986), Pete Wentz (1979), Nick Kroll (1978), Mark Wahlberg (1971), Ron Livingston (1967), Rick Riordan (1964), Kathleen Kennedy (1953), Ken Follett (1949)

June 6th

Ryan Higa (1990), Natalie Morales (1972), Paul Giamatti (1967), Jason Isaacs (1963), Colin Quinn (1959), Björn Borg (1956), Sukarno, First President of Indonesia (1901), Thomas Mann (1875)

June 7th

George Ezra (1993), Emily Ratajkowski (1991), Iggy Azalea (1990), Michael Cera (1988), Anna Kournikova (1981), Bill Hader (1978), Bear Grylls (1974), Prince (1958), Liam Neeson (1952), Tom Jones (1940)

June 8th

Rosanna Pansino (1985), Javier Mascherano (1984), Kanye West (1977), Shilpa Shetty (1975), Julianna Margulies (1966), Tim Berners-Lee (1955), Bonnie Tyler (1951), Nancy Sinatra (1940), Joan Rivers (1933), Jerry Stiller (1927), Barbara Bush (1925)

June 9th

Tanya Burr (1989), Mae Whitman (1988), Natalie Portman (1981), Matt Bellamy (1978), Miroslav Klose (1978), Johnny Depp (1963), Michael J. Fox (1961), Aaron Sorkin (1961)

June 10th

Kate Upton (1992), Faith Evans (1973), Bill Burr (1968), Elizabeth Hurley (1965), Jeanne Tripplehorn (1963), Carlo Ancelotti (1959), Judy Garland (1922), Prince Philip, Duke of Edinburgh (1921)

June 11th

Kodak Black (1997), Claire Holt (1988), Shia LaBeouf (1986), Joshua Jackson (1978), Peter Dinklage (1969), Hugh Laurie (1959), Gene Wilder (1933), Jacques Cousteau (1910)

June 12th

Philippe Coutinho (1992), Dave Franco (1985), Kendra Wilkinson (1985), Adriana Lima (1981), Richard Ayoade (1977), Lil Duval (1977), Anne Frank (1929), U.S President George H. W. Bush (1924)

June 13th

Aaron Taylor-Johnson (1990), Kat Dennings (1986), Mary-Kate and Ashley Olsen (1986), DJ Snake (1986), Chris Evans (1981), Steve-O (1974), Tim Allen (1953), Stellan Skarsgård (1951), W. B. Yeats (1865)

June 14th

Jesy Nelson (1991), Lucy Hale (1989), Torrance Coombs (1983), Alan Carr (1976), Steffi Graf (1969), Boy George (1961), U.S President Donald Trump (1946), Che Guevara (1928)

June 15th
Mohamed Salah (1992), Neil Patrick Harris (1973), Leah
Remini (1970), Ice Cube (1969), Courteney Cox (1964),
Helen Hunt (1963), Xi Jinping, General Secretary of the
Communist Party of China (1953), Erik Erikson (1902)

June 16th
John Newman (1990), Fernando Muslera (1986), Daniel
Brühl (1978), Eddie Cibrian (1973), John Cho (1972),
Tupac Shakur (1971), Jürgen Klopp (1967), Stan Laurel
(1890), Geronimo (1829)

June 17th
Kendrick Lamar (1987), Marie Avgeropoulos (1986), Venus
Williams (1980), Sven Nys (1976), Tory Burch (1966), Greg
Kinnear (1963), Barry Manilow (1943), Maurits Cornelis
Escher (1898), Igor Stravinsky (1882)

June 18th
Willa Holland (1991), Pierre-Emerick Aubameyang (1989),
Josh Dun (1988), Richard Madden (1986), Blake Shelton
(1976), Isabella Rossellini (1952), Paul McCartney (1942),
Delia Smith (1941), Barack Obama Sr. (1936)

June 19th

KSI (1993), Macklemore (1983), Aidan Turner (1983), Zoe Saldana (1978), Boris Johnson (1964), Laura Ingraham (1963), Paula Abdul (1962), Salman Rushdie (1947), Aung San Suu Kyi (1945)

June 20th

Christopher Mintz-Plasse (1989), Mike Birbiglia (1978), Quinton Jackson (1978), Frank Lampard (1978), Roy Nelson (1976), Mateusz Morawiecki, Prime Minister of Poland (1968), Nicole Kidman (1967), John Goodman (1952), Lionel Richie (1949), Brian Wilson (1942)

June 21st

Lana Del Rey (1985), Prince William, Duke of Cambridge (1982), Brandon Flowers (1981), Chris Pratt (1979), Juliette Lewis (1973), Joko Widodo, President of Indonesia (1961), Michel Platini (1955), Benazir Bhutto, Former Prime Minister of Pakistan (1953)